Saving Costs in Chemicals Management

HOW THE OECD ENSURES BENEFITS TO SOCIETY

This document, as well as any data and any map included herein, are without prejudice to the status of or sovereignty over any territory, to the delimitation of international frontiers and boundaries and to the name of any territory, city or area.

Please cite this publication as:
OECD (2019), *Saving Costs in Chemicals Management: How the OECD Ensures Benefits to Society*, OECD Publishing, Paris.
https://doi.org/10.1787/9789264311718-en

ISBN 978-92-64-31170-1 (print)
ISBN 978-92-64-31171-8 (pdf)

Photo credits: Cover © Suwit Ngaokaew/Shutterstock.com

Corrigenda to OECD publications may be found on line at: *www.oecd.org/about/publishing/corrigenda.htm*.

© OECD 2019

About the OECD

The Organisation for Economic Co-operation and Development (OECD) is an intergovernmental organisation in which representatives of 36 industrialised countries in North and South America, Europe and the Asia and Pacific region, as well as the European Commission, meet to co-ordinate and harmonise policies, discuss issues of mutual concern, and work together to respond to international problems. Most of the OECD's work is carried out by more than 200 specialised committees and working groups composed of member country delegates. Observers from several countries with special status at the OECD, and from interested international organisations, attend many of the OECD's workshops and other meetings. Committees and working groups are served by the OECD Secretariat, located in Paris, France, which is organised into directorates and divisions. The Environment, Health and Safety Division publishes free-of-charge documents in twelve different series: Testing and Assessment; Good Laboratory Practice and Compliance Monitoring; Pesticides; Biocides; Risk Management; Harmonisation of Regulatory Oversight in Biotechnology; Safety of Novel Foods and Feeds; Chemical Accidents; Pollutant Release and Transfer Registers; Emission Scenario Documents; Safety of Manufactured Nanomaterials; and Adverse Outcome Pathways. More information about the Environment, Health and Safety Programme and EHS publications is available on the OECD's World Wide Web site (www.oecd.org/chemicalsafety/).

Foreword

For more than 40 years, the OECD Environment, Health and Safety (EHS) Programme has been dedicated to helping governments develop and implement high-quality chemicals management policies and instruments to promote chemical safety worldwide. OECD countries now have science-based, rigorous and comprehensive systems for assessing and managing the risks of chemicals. But implementation of such regulatory systems can be time-consuming and expensive, which is why OECD countries work together to combine their skills and knowledge, avoid duplication of testing, minimise non-tariff distortions to trade, and ultimately be more efficient and effective in managing chemicals.

This report is the third in a series of reports that have quantified the financial benefits that accrue to governments and industry from the work of the EHS Programme. The first report, *Savings to governments and industry resulting from the OECD Environment, Health and Safety Programme*, was published in 1998 and estimated that the cost savings to industry and governments was approximately EUR 90 million a year (all monetary figures in this report have been adjusted for inflation). The second report, *Cutting Costs in Chemicals Management: How OECD Helps Governments and Industry*, was published in 2010 and estimated that the savings had grown to EUR 177 million per year.

This report explores a larger part of the work of the EHS Programme than the previous reports did, and details the significant savings it has secured for both governments and industry – more than EUR 309 million a year. These quantifiable savings only tell part of the story; the report also describes the programme's equally important non-quantifiable benefits (e.g. harmonising biotechnology safety assessments as a direct result of EHS work). Further, the estimated savings are just a snapshot of the benefits that accrue today, and this figure is expected to rise as the results of more EHS projects become available in the coming years.

This document was approved and published under the responsibility of the Joint Meeting of the Chemicals Committee and the Working Party on Chemicals, Pesticides and Biotechnology".

Acknowledgements

For this update of the 2010 report *Cutting Costs in Chemicals Managament: How the OECD Helps Governments and Industry*, a steering group was established with representatives from Colombia, the European Commission, Italy, the Netherlands, the United Kingdom, the industrial chemicals and pesticides industries, the consulting firm RPA and the OECD Secretariat.

The report was co-written by Richard Sigman and Marit Hjort from the OECD Secretariat, with the support of Walid Oueslati, Christiana Oladini-James, Yukie Saegusa and Hannah Thabet, also from the Secretariat, along with the editing contribution of Jennifer Allain. Valuable input was also provided by Andrew Gray (Medicines and Healthcare Products Regulatory Agency, United Kingdom), Joop de Knecht (National Institute for Public Health and Environment, the Netherlands), Emily Sanchez and Kevin Swift from the American Chemistry Council, Steve Smith from SC Johnson, Craig Dunlop from Syngenta and Marco Camboni, Meg Postle, Anthony Footitt and Liam Wakefield from RPA.

Table of contents

Tables

Figures

Boxes

Follow OECD Publications on:

http://twitter.com/OECD_Pubs

http://www.facebook.com/OECDPublications

http://www.linkedin.com/groups/OECD-Publications-4645871

http://www.youtube.com/oecdilibrary

http://www.oecd.org/oecddirect/

Acronyms and abbreviations

ACC	American Chemistry Council
BRIICS	Brazil, Russian Federation, India, Indonesia, China and South Africa
ECHA	European Chemicals Agency
EHS	Environment, Health and Safety
EU	European Union
GDP	Gross domestic product
GLP	Good Laboratory Practice
HPV	High Production Volume
IATA	Integrated Approaches to Testing and Assessment
KKDIK	*Kimyasalların Kaydı, Değerlendirmesi, İzni ve Kısıtlanması* (Turkish "REACH"-like regulation)
K-REACH	Korea's Act on the Registration and Evaluation of Chemicals
MAD	Mutual Acceptance of Data
NGO	Non-governmental organisation
OECD	Organisation for Economic Co-operation and Development
PCBs	Polychlorinated biphenyls
PFASs	Per- and polyfluoroalkyl substances
PRTR	Pollutant Release and Transfer Register
(Q)SAR	(Quantitative) Structure-Activity Relationship
REACH	Registration, Evaluation, Authorisation and Restriction of Chemicals
RPA	Risk & Policy Analysts Limited
SAICM	Strategic Approach to International Chemicals Management
SDG	Sustainable Development Goal
SIDS	Screening Information Data Set
TBT	Technical barrier to trade
USD	United States dollar
US EPA	United States Environmental Protection Agency
WTO	World Trade Organization

Executive summary

Governments are striving to design and implement cost-effective policies for "greener" and more innovative sources of growth and more sustainable consumption. How such policies are implemented in the chemical industry will be critical to achieving sustained success. This report discusses both the quantifiable and non-quantifiable benefits that accrue to governments and the chemical industry from the OECD Environment, Health and Safety (EHS) Programme.

The chemical industry is one of the world's largest industries, with products worth around USD 5 681 billion in 2017. OECD countries account for almost half of global production (42%). The OECD estimates that world production is expected to grow to almost USD 22 000 billion by 2060.

Modern life without chemicals would be inconceivable; chemicals are a part of our daily life. But given the potential environmental and human health risks from exposure to chemicals, governments have a major responsibility to ensure that chemicals are produced and used as safely as possible. Effective regulation should be based on a productive working relationship with the chemical industry in the public interest.

The potential risks of chemicals are managed in OECD countries through sophisticated and comprehensive science-based systems founded on the identification of hazards and the assessment of risks. The role of the OECD is to assist member countries to meet the dual aims of developing and implementing policies and high-quality instruments to protect human health and the environment and to make their systems and processes for managing chemicals as efficient as possible. In order to eliminate duplication of work and avoid non-tariff barriers to trade, emphasis has been on developing frameworks for work sharing in gathering and assessing information on the potential risks of chemicals. The time-tested instruments of the OECD Mutual Acceptance of Data (MAD) system provide the basis for generating savings to governments and industry. These savings are a measure of the success of OECD's work on chemicals, which is further demonstrated by the adherence of non-members to the MAD system.

The EHS Programme was set up to help OECD governments optimise the use of their resources, reduce non-tariff barriers to trade, and save industry time and money by co-operating to test and evaluate the safety of industrial chemicals, pesticides, biocides, nanomaterials and products of modern biotechnology. It does so through a variety of ways: harmonisation, burden sharing, exchanging technical and policy information, international co-operation, ensuring green growth, and contributing to sustainable development.

Key findings and conclusions

The net financial savings to governments and industry brought by the programme (after deducting costs) for harmonising the testing and assessment of new biocides, new and existing industrial chemicals, and pesticides, are estimated to be more than EUR 309 million a year.

This report estimates that net savings attributable to the EHS Programme have grown by 75% since 2010 and by over 240% since 1998. However, it is important to note that unlike the estimates for 2010 and 1998 that were documented in the two previous reports which quantified the financial benefits that accrue to governments and industry, the estimates in the present report include the significant savings from tests on biocides not being repeated due to MAD. Those savings are estimated to be around EUR 61 million per year. In addition, since 2010 there has been an increase in the number of OECD member countries and non-member full adherents to MAD. This means that the reduction in duplicative testing is now spread across more countries and hence the savings are greater.

Some activities within the EHS Programme can currently only be described in qualitative terms, either because the benefits are not easy to measure in direct monetary gains or because the activities have not been implemented for a sufficient length of time to gauge their impacts. However, these benefits are just as real and important as the quantifiable benefits. Many of them are due to countries working together to tackle chemicals management issues, thus sharing the burden associated with tasks that they otherwise might have to face alone. Such burden sharing saves valuable time and resources for government and industry.

Further, by pooling resources, OECD countries develop methods for improving the way risk assessments are conducted, which in turn leads to better risk management decisions. And, as some of the most experienced experts across the OECD participate in this work, countries get access to high-quality, globally respected material in many different technical areas. Individually, no country could match this level of expertise in each field. Finally, by harmonising chemical safety tools and policies, governments are provided with a common platform for collaboration.

Some examples of benefits which are due to work sharing under the EHS Programme include: facilitating easy access to information on chemicals, thus reducing the risks of duplicative testing and increasing the reuse of existing assessments by other countries; providing access to harmonised templates for structuring data when reporting summaries of the results from health and environmental safety tests; ensuring the safety of manufactured nanomaterials by developing harmonised tools for testing and assessment; harmonising the safety assessment methodologies for products of modern biotechnology; providing harmonised tools to identify endocrine disrupters; reducing the need for governmental inspections of test facilities in other countries that adhere to MAD as such countries can request another country to conduct an inspection of a test facility located in the other country; enhancing hazard assessment methods and limiting the use of animals in chemical testing; facilitating the exchange of information on chemical accidents to support prevention, preparedness and response; advancing harmonisation of biocides regulations; and counteracting the illegal trade of pesticides.

In addition, and most importantly, by working together through the EHS Programme, governments can better, and more rapidly, address and minimise impacts to health and the environment from the production and use of biocides, pesticides, industrial chemicals and manufactured nanomaterials.

Finally, while this report has not tried to quantify the annual savings for pharmaceutical companies, these savings are expected to be significant. Pharmaceutical companies conduct many non-clinical tests using OECD Test Guidelines and follow OECD Principles of Good Laboratory Practice, and, hence, many potential benefits could accrue to this industry as a result of MAD. On average, OECD governments review non-clinical test data from companies on around 34 new active ingredients per year. The testing of such compounds can be in the millions. As such products are marketed in multiple regions, there are likely to be great savings from the reduction in duplicative testing.

1. Introduction to the OECD Environment, Health and Safety Programme

This chapter explores the economic and environmental aspects associated with the chemical industry. It then discusses how the OECD Environment, Health and Safety (EHS) Programme helps OECD governments reduce barriers to trade, optimise the use of their resources, and save industry time and money by co-operating to test and evaluate the safety of biocides, industrial chemicals, pesticides and nanotechnology products. The chapter describes how the EHS Programme helps to achieve these goals through harmonisation, burden sharing, exchanging technical and policy information, international co-operation, ensuring green growth, and contributing to sustainable development.

1.1. Background

Governments today are striving to design and implement cost-effective policies for "greener" and more innovative sources of growth and more sustainable consumption. How such policies are implemented in the chemical industry will be critical to achieving sustained success. The chemical industry is one of the largest economic sectors in the world and contributes significantly to the living standards and health of people, but it also potentially has a negative impact on human health and the environment.

Given the potential environmental and health risks associated with the production, transport, use and disposal of chemicals, the sector is highly regulated. Regulations cost money – to both industry and governments. The fact that each OECD country has its own regulatory processes and requirements, with many of the same chemicals being involved and traded amongst them, means that much effort is potentially duplicated and time and money wasted.

It is for these reasons that the OECD's Environment, Health and Safety (EHS) Programme has been working for more than 40 years to harmonise chemical safety tools and policies. In addition to dealing with the safe use of industrial chemicals, manufactured nanomaterials, pesticides, biocides and products of modern biotechnology, the programme addresses related areas of concern and interest, such as chemical accidents and releases of hazardous chemicals and pollutants to the environment (e.g. by assisting countries to set up Pollutant Release and Transfer Registers). Its aim is to allow governments and industry to develop the most cost-effective approaches for protecting human health and the environment from the risks posed by chemicals, avoiding duplication of effort, and ensuring barriers to trade avoided.

Much of the EHS Programme's work is in line with the policy recommendations in the *OECD Environmental Outlook for 2050* (OECD, 2012a), which stress the need to intensify international co-operation in the management of chemicals, including by:

- sharing work on the assessment of chemicals and development of methodologies for assessing existing, emerging or poorly understood issues (e.g. endocrine disrupters, nanomaterials, per- and polyfluoroalkyl substances, and chemical mixtures)

- increasing the sustainable use of chemicals and green chemistry

- implementing policies to protect the most vulnerable human life stages (i.e. early life).

This chapter explores the economic and environmental aspects associated with the chemical industry. It then discusses how the OECD's EHS Programme helps OECD governments reduce barriers to trade, optimise the use of their resources, and save industry time and money – more than EUR 309 million[1] – by co-operating to test and evaluate the safety of biocides, industrial chemicals, pesticides, biotechnology and nanotechnology products. The chapter describes how the EHS Programme helps to achieve these goals through harmonisation, burden sharing, exchanging technical and policy information, international co-operation, ensuring green growth, and contributing to sustainable development.

1.2. The chemical industry

The chemical industry – which includes producers of industrial chemicals, polymers, pharmaceuticals, pesticides, biocides, food and feed additives, and cosmetics – is one of the world's largest industrial sectors. Every manmade material is made of, or contains, one or more of the thousands of chemicals produced by the industry each year, from paints and insect spray to computers, kitchen appliances, medicines or sun cream. The industry is a major employer, with 3.3 million jobs in the EU chemical industry (including pharmaceuticals, rubber and plastic) and up to three times as many indirect jobs generated by this sector (Cefic, 2018). The US chemical industry (excluding pharmaceuticals) employs 529 000 people, with each job generating an additional 7.1 jobs in other sectors of the economy, such as retail trade and health care (ACC, 2018).

The chemical industry is very diverse, comprising basic or commodity chemicals (e.g. inorganic chemicals, petrochemicals, petrochemical derivatives); speciality chemicals derived from basic chemicals (e.g. adhesives and sealants, catalysts, coatings, plastic additives); products derived from life sciences (e.g. pharmaceuticals and pesticides); and consumer care products (e.g. soap, detergents, bleaches, hair and skin care products, and fragrances).

Starting from the early days of the EHS Programme, the world's chemical industry has grown in value more than ten-fold, from approximately USD 520 billion in 1978 to USD 5 681 billion in 2017 (including pharmaceuticals) (ACC, 2018). OECD countries accounted for an estimated 42% of global chemical production in 2017.[2] The value of the chemical industry has increased by 33% since the last time the OECD took stock of the costs and savings of the EHS Programme in 2010, and by a total of 132% since the first time the Organisation carried out a similar exercise, which was in 1998 (Figure 1.1). Over the period 2020-60, the OECD estimates that total world production of chemicals will increase to USD 21 748 billion (OECD, 2019).

Figure 1.1. **Annual global sales of the chemical industry**

Billion USD

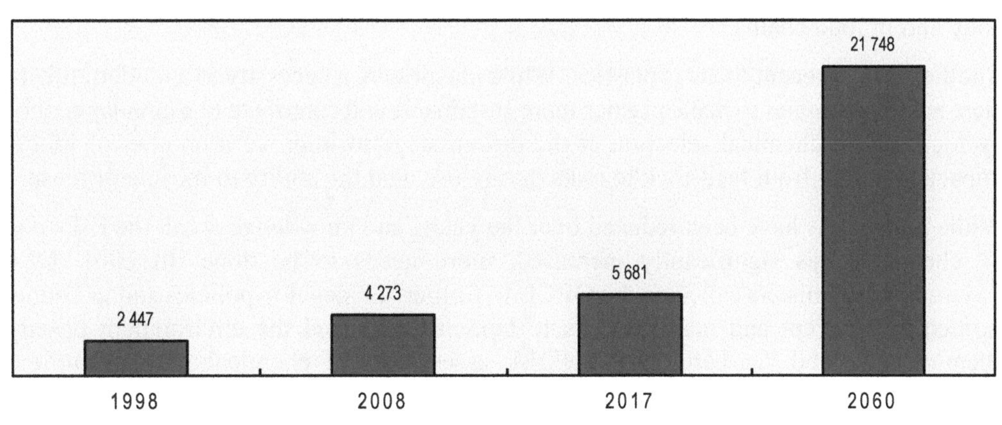

Sources: ACC (2018), *2017 Guide to the Business of Chemistry*; OECD (2019), *Global Materials Resources Outlook to 2060: Economic Drivers and Environmental Consequences*, www.oecd.org/publications/global-material-resources-outlook-to-2060-9789264307452-en.htm

The chemical industry is a major component of world trade, with global chemical exports in 2017 (excluding pharmaceuticals) accounting for USD 1 415.6 billion (ACC, 2018). The chemical industry also constitutes a significant part of GDP in many countries. In 2016, 25% of US GDP was supported by the chemical industry (ACC, 2017).

1.3. Use of chemicals: Benefits to society but also potential risks to human health and the environment

Chemicals have a wide variety of applications and can improve people's health and well-being. For instance, pharmaceuticals have played a major role in increasing life expectancy, and agrochemicals can improve crop yields. Further, research in "sustainable chemistry"[3] has allowed safer and less hazardous substances to be developed for a number of uses. For example, the development of polymeric flame retardants has allowed for less hazardous and still efficient firefighting foam. Further, products such as insulation material and low temperature detergents can improve energy efficiency to help combat climate change, while nanocomposites can remove metals from smokestack emissions. Still other products, such as those that prevent and cure disease or improve crop yields, can improve people's lives, and manufactured nanomaterials are already revolutionising the way we produce certain types of goods such as electronic equipment, tyres, clothes and medicines. In addition, new business models such as service-oriented chemical leasing aim to reduce consumption of chemicals.

However, the production and use of chemicals can also have a negative impact on human health and the environment. Although the impacts are complex and sometimes open to scientific debate, some deleterious effects are well documented, such as those toxic chemicals that persist in the environment and that are bioaccumulative[4] (e.g. dichlorodiphenyltrichloroethane [DDT], dioxins, and polychlorinated biphenyls [PCBs])[5]. The use of nanomaterials also poses new challenges with identifying potential unintended risks to humans and the environment. Furthermore, concern has been raised about the impact of endocrine-disrupting substances on human reproduction and development (OECD, 2018a). Per- and polyfluoroalkyl substances (PFASs) form another group of contaminants of global concern, due to the demonstrated behaviour, persistency and toxicological profile of certain PFASs, as well as their potential to accumulate in the body and in food chains.[6]

Another area of recent focus is plastics. While plastics are a necessity to a modern lifestyle, there are opportunities to make plastics more sustainable and contribute to a circular economy by focusing on chemical selection at the design stage to improve a number of lifecycle impacts, ranging from feedstock to risks during use, and the ability to recycle or reuse.

While many risks have been reduced over the years, and knowledge about the risks posed by chemicals has significantly increased, more needs to be done. In 2001, OECD Environment Ministers called on the OECD to further "… develop policies and instruments to identify, prevent and manage risks to human health and the environment posed by chemicals …" and "… harmonise the risk assessment of chemicals, for example, by developing criteria for identifying inherently unsafe chemicals (e.g. for persistence, bioaccumulation, toxicity), developing new testing and assessment methods, in particular for endocrine disrupters, and expanding the Mutual Acceptance of Data" (OECD, 2001). More recently, one of the key conclusions of the *OECD Environmental Outlook to 2050*, endorsed by OECD Environment Ministers in 2012, was that:

... while OECD governments continue to make good progress collecting and assessing information on human exposure to individual chemicals throughout their lifecycle, knowledge gaps still exist concerning the health effects from thousands of chemicals present in the environment. More information on potential exposures to chemicals in products and in the environment, as well as the adverse effects of combined human exposure to multiple chemicals is needed. (OECD, 2012).

1.4. Why governments work together to tackle the risks posed by chemicals

1.4.1. Impacts of a non-harmonised approach to chemical regulation and testing

Today, OECD governments have comprehensive regulatory frameworks for preventing and/or minimising the health and environmental risks posed by chemicals. Indeed, the chemical industry is one of the most regulated of all industries. The objective of regulatory frameworks is to ensure that chemical products already on the market are safe or managed in a safe way, and that new ones are properly assessed before being placed on the market. This is done by either testing specific chemicals to determine their behaviour in the environment and their toxicity in mammals and other organisms or by using predictive models, such as read-across or (Quantitative) Structure-Activity Relationships ([Q]SARs) (see Box 2.2), analysing the results, and taking appropriate action.

Such a framework, while rigorous and comprehensive, is very resource-intensive and time-consuming for both governments and industry. For instance, the cost for a pesticide company to test one new active ingredient for health and environmental effects is, on average, EUR 21.5 million,[7] and the time needed for a government to review and assess the data is around 1.95 person-years.[8] For emerging technologies, such as biotechnology and manufactured nanomaterials, the development of new test methods and regulatory approaches for safety assessment can be particularly burdensome and costly.

As many of the same chemicals are produced in more than one OECD country (or are traded across countries), different national chemical control policies can lead to duplication in testing and government assessment, thereby wasting the resources of industry and government alike. Different national policies also create non-tariff or technical barriers to trade (TBT) in chemicals. In 2018, the OECD's Trade and Agriculture Directorate issued a working paper demonstrating that, on average, the cost (*ad valorem* equivalent) of technical barriers in chemicals was 9.3% of the unit value (OECD, 2018b). Further, preliminary evidence from OECD research indicates that trade agreements that include mutual recognition and harmonisation of TBT measures, including mutual recognition of TBT conformity assessment procedures, have a positive influence on chemical trade flows, presumably by reducing trade costs associated with these non-tariff measures. Over the period 2015-17, as much as 26% of specific trade concerns raised in the World Trade Organization's (WTO) Technical Barriers to Trade Committee referred to measures citing environmental protection among their objectives.[9] Of all the environment-related measures identified in notifications to the WTO between 2009 and 2016, 18% had to do with either "chemical, toxic and hazardous substances management" or "ozone layer protection". Half of these were TBT measures.[10]

Furthermore, differences in regulations and test standards discourage research, innovation and growth, and increase the time it takes to introduce a new (and potentially safer) product onto the market. They also lead to inefficiencies for governments, because authorities cannot take full advantage of the work done by others which would help reduce the resources needed for chemicals control.

1.4.2. Benefits of the OECD Environment, Health and Safety Programme

In order to make the process of testing and evaluation of chemicals as efficient and cost effective as possible for governments and industry while maintaining a high level of health and environmental protection, OECD countries agree on overall policies; develop harmonised instruments for their implementation; and set frameworks for, and participate in, work-sharing at the OECD.

The OECD is particularly well-suited to developing common tools and policies for chemicals for several reasons:

- OECD countries account for close to half of the world's production of chemicals (approximately 42%)[11], giving them an important global responsibility for the sound management of an industry that includes many large multinational companies.

- OECD countries have similar markets, populations, per capita gross domestic product (GDP) and levels of environmental protection, greatly facilitating the development and use of common approaches.

- All OECD countries are seeking ways to reduce government spending without compromising economic development, trade, or human health and environmental safety. By working together through the OECD, governments can ensure that sound management of chemical products is implemented in a way that is most efficient for them and for industry.

The EHS Programme was set up to help OECD governments reduce barriers to trade, optimise the use of their resources, and save industry time and money by co-operating to test and evaluate the safety of biocides, industrial chemicals, pesticides, biotechnology and nanotechnology products. The programme achieves these goals through harmonisation, burden sharing, exchanging technical and policy information, international co-operation, ensuring green growth, and contributing to sustainable development. Each of these are described in turn below.

1.4.3. Harmonisation

If national approaches to chemical regulation are harmonised, industry is not faced with a plethora of conflicting or duplicative requirements, making it easier for companies to place a product on the market and thus stimulating competition. Further, governments are provided with a common basis for working with each other, and non-tariff barriers to trade are reduced. The principal tools for harmonisation are a set of OECD Council Decisions that make up the OECD Mutual Acceptance of Data (MAD) system,[12] including the *OECD Guidelines for the Testing of Chemicals* and the *OECD Principles of Good Laboratory Practice* (GLP) (OECD, 1998). The MAD system helps to avoid conflicting or duplicative national requirements, provides a common basis for co-operation among national authorities, and avoids creating non-tariff barriers to trade. In endorsing these Decisions, OECD countries have agreed that a safety test carried out in accordance with the *OECD Test Guidelines* and *OECD Principles of Good Laboratory Practice* in one OECD country must be accepted by other OECD countries for assessment purposes. This saves the chemical industry the expense of duplicate testing for products that are marketed in more than one country. In addition, the MAD system significantly reduces the number of animals needed for testing. The Test Guidelines and GLP Principles are continuously expanded and updated to ensure they are state-of-the-art.

A 1997 Council Decision also sets out a procedure for non-OECD economies to adhere to this system and to participate in the development of Test Guidelines and Principles of GLP, which have long formed the basis of national technical regulations related to non-clinical health and environmental safety data acceptance in OECD countries. This fulfils the major World Trade Organization (WTO) requirements for "international standards" of transparency, avoidance of trade barriers and openness of participation by all WTO members.

Box 1.1. **Benefits of Mutual Acceptance of Data for industry**

Because of MAD, sponsors don't have to assume an excess uncertainty factor in planning future resources.

– Japan Pharmaceutical Manufacturers Association

Given the expansion of testing that is required in the ecological/non-target organism area of the data requirements for pesticides, the impact of OECD Test Guidelines is significant. Our view is that acceptance of the OECD GLP-generated data is a key consideration in determining in which countries registration will be sought, therefore having a significant impact on the crop protection tools that are available in direct relationship with the Mutual Acceptance of Data principles and the acceptance of OECD GLP data. Because of this direct relationship, increasing the number of countries that are members of the OECD, or have agreements that enable the recognition and acceptance of OECD GLP data, is critically important to industry, agriculture and consumers.

– A pesticides company based in an OECD country

The cost savings from the MAD system and the continuous development of new and updated Test Guidelines and additional guidance on GLP and compliance monitoring are major benefits of the EHS Programme. Every year, many companies submit notifications or registration applications for hundreds of new industrial chemicals, biocides and pesticides. As described below, the savings to the pesticides, biocides and industrial chemicals sectors for testing new substances are more than EUR 317 million each year, if the cost of participation in the EHS Programme is excluded. This does not include the savings for testing of existing chemicals as well as other types of chemicals (e.g. pharmaceuticals, many of which are subject to non-clinical health and safety testing using OECD Test Guidelines and GLP Principles). Furthermore, animal suffering is significantly reduced as a test only needs to be conducted once. Over the last few years, the number of OECD member countries and non-member MAD adherents has increased, thereby facilitating greater harmonisation and reducing the number of potentially different new national standards for safety assessments and further increasing the savings.[13]

1.4.4. Sharing the burden

By working together to tackle chemical management issues, countries can share the workload. This saves valuable government and industry resources and allows more to be achieved more quickly. For example, through the OECD's Programme on High Production Volume (HPV) chemicals, which was concluded in 2014, the burden of testing and evaluating the safety of these substances was shared among countries according to the number of HPV chemicals produced and imported by each country (OECD, 2013). This programme lead to the generation of hazard assessments agreed by all member countries for 1 343 chemicals. This collaborative approach saved considerable resources for governments, experts and industry (OECD, 2010).

> Box 1.2. **Benefits of harmonised test methods for industry**
>
> *Data following OECD Test Guidelines are more readily accepted, timely and relevant – the input of the national experts from member countries is highly regarded and widely recognised in helping eliminate what otherwise would be several rounds of submission and comments following protocol development. With the expert input in the test method design (application of OECD Guidance Documents 1 and 34, e.g. the Solna Principles), there is more confidence in the outcome of OECD studies. Similarly, the GLP programme provides confidence in the repeatability of studies.*
>
> *Further, harmonised test methods allow for proposals like Review Sharing of Acute Studies[1] (vs. work sharing) to be put forward. Review sharing, even with some fixed level of auditing, would free up significant resources for government agencies permitting limited specialist resources to work on higher value added activities such as risk assessment. If an Acute Toxicology 6 Pack[2] is sent to 30 OECD member countries, the result would be 180 reviews, 174 of which are redundant and add no value to the consumer we are all trying to protect. This level of calibration is only possible with the use of OECD Test Guidelines.*
>
> *Lastly, harmonised test methods facilitate the comparison of different formulations against the same standard test, which is helpful for decision making.*
>
> – Representative of a biocide company based in an OECD country
>
> *Several years ago one country proposed to develop its own pesticide toxicology test guidelines, until it realised it had to use OECD test guidelines. If it had developed its own unique guidelines, our members may have had to conduct additional tests which could have required unnecessary animal testing, increased costs both to the regulator and to our members, and additional, needless bureaucracy.*
>
> – CropLife International
>
> *Notes:* 1. Review Sharing of Acute Studies is organised by the OECD Biocides Programme (see Chapter 3).
> 2. Acute Toxicology 6 Pack is a US standard requirement for pesticides and biocides.

While there are thousands of chemicals on the market today, only a relatively small number are produced in large volumes. In the European Union, for example, four substances account for 36.1% of the total volume of chemicals produced or imported. Substances manufactured and imported in quantities over 1 million tonnes per year (i.e. 229 substances) account for over 96% of the total volume (see the three largest categories in Figure 1.2. Under the HPV Chemicals Programme, the OECD published a list of chemicals that were produced or imported at levels greater than 1 000 tonnes per year in at least one member country/region (OECD, 2007). As, in general, the higher the volume, the greater the potential exposure to humans and releases to the environment, such large volume chemicals are likely to be prioritised by countries for assessments. As these large commodity chemicals are produced in multiple countries, there are great opportunities for OECD countries to work together on such assessments. Similarly, by sharing approaches for these chemicals using common risk assessment methodologies, companies that produce and market these chemicals in multiple countries can reduce their costs when they are assessed by multiple countries. Costs are further reduced by allowing predictive models to be used for groups of similar chemicals so that each chemical does not have to be individually tested.

Figure 1.2. **Proportion of total EU chemical production by tonnage band**

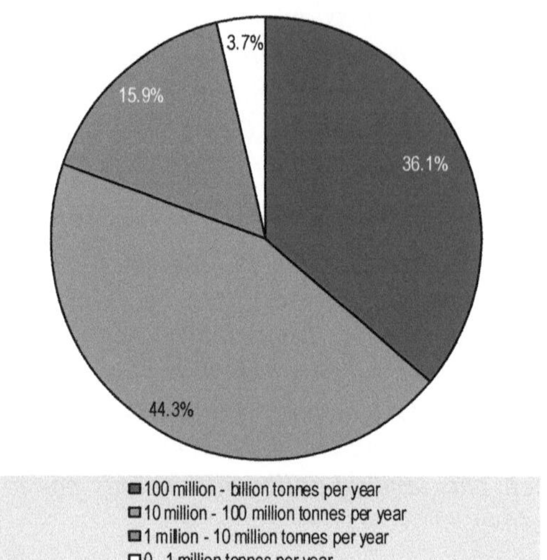

Source: Based on data published by the European Chemicals Agency (n.d.), "REACH registration results", https://echa.europa.eu/reach-registrations-since-2008 (accessed 31 August 2018).

1.4.5. Exchange of technical and policy information

The EHS Programme provides a forum for countries to exchange technical and policy information. This creates greater confidence in, and acceptance of, each other's approaches, and ultimately fosters more efficient, effective and more closely harmonised national chemicals management programmes. For example, it is estimated that reviewing a full industry dossier on a new pesticide and writing a comprehensive report (monograph) takes a government 1.95 person-years. However, by using another country's monograph for the same pesticide – based on the OECD monograph format – government experts estimate that 1.02 full person-years of time would be saved (i.e. 52%)[14], thus generating significant savings. By discussing their chemical control policies together and seeking ways to harmonise instruments and methods, countries tend to develop similar policies and regulations. This, in turn, means that government regulators who exchange assessments can significantly reduce the time and effort needed to approve a new product or (re-)register an existing one. In this way, not only do governments save resources, products can also be brought to the market faster. Finally, governments have access to the experience of the many scientific and policy experts from other governments, industry, and academia who participate in the work of the EHS Programme.

1.4.6. International co-operation

OECD countries currently account for most of the world's production of chemicals; however, their share of the global market dropped from close to 75% in 2008 (OECD, 2008b) to 42% in 2017[15], and is expected to decrease further by 2060 as production in non-OECD economies – particularly Brazil, the Russian Federation, India, Indonesia, People's Republic of China (hereafter: China) and South Africa (BRIICS) – increases rapidly (OECD, 2019). The BRIICS countries' share in global chemical markets was 13%

in 2000 (OECD, 2012) and is expected to grow to 38% in 2020 (OECD, 2019). Some of this increase has been due to the lower costs associated with production in the BRIICS, but also with the need for facilities to be closer to final markets and feedstock sources (OECD, 2012; UNEP, 2013). In addition, technology transfer from companies in developed countries to emerging economies – due to, among other things, joint ventures and mergers and acquisitions – has helped emerging economies innovate and play a larger role in the global market (Kiriyama, 2010).

Chinese companies in particular are active in gaining access to advanced technologies in partnership with multinationals, alongside in-house research and development (Kiriyama, 2010). According to OECD estimates, China's share in global chemical production was 22% in 2011 and 26% – with a total value of USD 2 188 billion – in 2018 (OECD, 2019). The share of other Asian countries and of Latin America also increased. Africa's contribution to global chemical production remains small, but the chemicals sector is expected to play an increasingly important role in the economies of specific African countries, notably South Africa – a full adherent to MAD – which has the continent's largest chemical industry, accounting for about 5% of GDP (UNEP, 2013).

With the rapid expansion of the chemical industry in non-member economies, which could increase the potential for risks to human health and the environment, greater international co-operation with these economies will be needed to build capacity, share information and promote effective chemical management globally. Co-operation will also be necessary to ensure that new national chemical management systems do not lead to duplicative testing and assessments or to new trade barriers.

The EHS Programme has a proactive outreach strategy to encourage the participation of non-member countries in the work of the programme. This allows non-members to profit from access to technical and policy discussions and documentation, while member countries and industry profit from greater convergence of environment, health and safety programmes around the world. As a result of the EHS Programme's outreach strategy, the following non-member countries are full adherents to MAD and have the same opportunity to benefit from this system as OECD countries: Argentina, Brazil, India, Malaysia, Singapore and South Africa.

Further, the OECD has played a key role in implementing Chapter 19 of Agenda 21[16] on the sound management of toxic chemicals. Its EHS Programme is one of the leading international programmes in the field and its products are used widely by non-member countries. The Programme is increasingly involved with non-member countries and with other Participating Organisations of the Inter-Organization Programme for the Sound Management of Chemicals (IOMC), to promote the global harmonisation of methods and approaches assisting countries in the development and implementation of their national industrial chemicals management systems (SAICM, 2018). These efforts can ensure increased savings from the EHS Programme to governments and industry.

In 2008, the OECD Council adopted a Resolution on the Implementation of the UN Strategic Approach to International Chemicals Management (SAICM) (OECD, 2008a). This Resolution calls for countries to work together through the OECD to ensure that as chemicals management programmes are established or upgraded, OECD products will be accessible, relevant and useful to non-members to help them develop their capacities for managing chemicals. The OECD is working on over 40% of the 273 activities listed in the SAICM Global Plan of Action, and contributes to the implementation of multiple work plans on emerging policy issues and other issues of concern that have been adopted by the International Conference on Chemicals Management (ICCM).

1.4.7. Ensuring green growth

The chemical industry and green innovation mutually benefit each other, as: the chemical industry and chemicals management represent scientific disciplines that influence innovation in green technologies; and green innovation plays a crucial role for the future of the chemical industry. The EHS Programme can help "green" the approaches governments take to economic growth by reducing the overall costs associated with the protection of health and the environment. Notably, the EHS Programme reduces the costs of notification of new chemicals, thereby reducing the barriers to innovation. Further, the programme allows for more existing chemicals to be assessed, potentially leading to more substitutions.

The EHS Programme contributes to the implementation of the OECD's Green Growth Strategy, *Towards Green Growth* (OECD, 2011a), through, among other things, its work on integrated pest management, the sustainable use of manufactured nanomaterials, substitution of hazardous substances and predicting the properties of chemicals without animal testing. Some of the programme's contributions to green growth are demonstrated in *Fostering Innovation for Green Growth* (OECD, 2011b), which addresses innovation as an important driver of the transition towards green growth, and *Sustainable Chemistry: Evidence on Innovation from Patent Data* (OECD, 2011c), which uses patent data to investigate green chemistry innovation trends.

1.4.8. Contributing to sustainable development

The EHS Programme helps achieve progress towards many of the UN Sustainable Development Goals (SDGs).[17] Its work on risk assessment and risk management methodologies is applicable to any type of chemical and any stage in its lifecycle, independent of their use, and addresses environmental protection for all media as well as worker and consumer safety, including the safety of children. This work therefore not only contributes to meeting SDG 12 on responsible consumption and production, and specifically Target 12.4 on the sound management of chemicals and waste, but also to Target 3.9 on reducing deaths from pollution, Target 6.3 on water quality and Target 9.4 on sustainable industries.

In addition, a number of specific programmes contribute to other SDG targets:

- The programme on pesticides and sustainable pest control contributes to Target 2.4 on sustainable food production systems and resilient agricultural practices.

- The programme on chemical accident prevention, preparedness and response contributes to Target 11.5 on reducing the number of deaths, the number of people affected and the direct economic losses relative to global GDP caused by disasters.

- The programme on Pollutant, Release and Transfer Registers (PRTRs), in addition to contributing to pollution reduction, facilitates the tracking of progress towards Target 12.5, which sets out to "substantially reduce waste generation through prevention, reduction, recycling and reuse".

Notes

1   See Chapter 2.

2.   Figure provided by the ACC.

3.   Sustainable chemistry is a scientific concept that seeks to improve the efficiency with which natural resources are used to meet human needs for chemical products and services.

4.   Bioaccumulation refers to the gradual accumulation of substances, such as pesticides or other organic chemicals, in an organism and in the food chain.

5.   See the Stockholm Convention website at: http://chm.pops.int/TheConvention/ThePOPs/The12InitialPOPs/tabid/296/Default.aspx.

6.   See the OECD Portal on Per and Poly Fluorinated Chemicals at: www.oecd.org/chemicalsafety/portal-perfluorinated-chemicals.

7.   Based on the EHS survey of industry (2018). See Annex A for details.

8.   Based on the EHS survey of governments (2018). See Annex A for details.

9.   See the World Trade Organization's Technical Barriers to Trade Information Management System, available at: http://tbtims.wto.org/en/SpecificTradeConcerns/Search.

10.   See the World Trade Organization's *Environmental Database*, available at: www.wto.org/english/tratop_e/envir_e/envdb_e.htm.

11.   Figure provided by the ACC.

12.   The OECD Instruments for Ensuring Mutual Acceptance of Data are available at: www.oecd.org/chemicalsafety/testing/council-acts-on-mutual-acceptance-of-data.htm.

13.   Non member MAD adherents include Argentina, Brazil, India, Malaysia, Singapore, and South Africa.

14.   Based on the EHS survey of governments (2018). See Annex A for details.

15.   Figure provided by the ACC.

16.   Agenda 21, adopted by more than 178 governments at the United Nations Conference on Environment and Development held in Rio de Janerio (Brazil) in 1992, is a comprehensive plan of action to address human impacts on the environment.

17.   The 17 SDGs were adopted by the 193 countries of the United Nation's General Assembly in September 2015. Each of these goals has specific targets to be achieved by 2030.

References

ACC (2018), *2018 Guide to the Business of Chemistry*, American Chemistry Council, Arlington, Virginia.

ACC (2017), *2017 Guide to the Business of Chemistry*, American Chemistry Council, Arlington, Virginia.

Cefic (2018), *Facts and Figures of the European Chemical Industry*, http://www.cefic.org/Facts-and-Figures/.

European Chemicals Agency (n.d.), "REACH registration results", https://echa.europa.eu/reach-registrations-since-2008 (accessed 31 August 2018).

Kiriyama, N. (2010), "Trade and innovation: Report on the chemicals sector", *OECD Trade Policy Working Papers*, No. 103, OECD Publishing, Paris, https://doi.org/10.1787/5km69t4hmr6c-en.

OECD (2019), *Global Materials Resources Outlook to 2060: Economic Drivers and Environmental Consequences*, OECD Publishing, Paris, www.oecd.org/publications/global-material-resources-outlook-to-2060-9789264307452-en.htm.

OECD (2018a), "OECD work on endocrine disrupting chemicals", OECD Publishing, Paris, www.oecd.org/env/ehs/testing/oecdworkrelatedtoendocrinedisrupters.htm.

OECD (2018b), "Estimating ad-valorem equivalent of non-tariff measures: Combining price-based and quantity-based approaches", TAD/TC/WP(2017)12/FINAL, OECD Publishing, Paris, www.oecd.org/officialdocuments/publicdisplaydocumentpdf/?cote=TAD/TC/WP(2017)12/FINAL&docLanguage=En.

OECD (2013), "The OECD Cooperative Chemicals Assessment Programme: An international programme with global reach", brochure, OECD, Paris, www.oecd.org/env/ehs/risk-assessment/CoCAP-flyer.pdf.

OECD (2012), *OECD Environmental Outlook to 2050: The Consequences of Inaction*, OECD Publishing, Paris, https://doi.org/10.1787/9789264122246-en.

OECD (2011a), *Towards Green Growth*, OECD Green Growth Studies, OECD Publishing, Paris, https://doi.org/10.1787/9789264111318-en.

OECD (2011b), *Fostering Innovation for Green Growth*, OECD Green Growth Studies, OECD Publishing, Paris, http://dx.doi.org/10.1787/9789264119925-en.

OECD (2011c), *Sustainable Chemistry: Evidence on Innovation from Patent Data*, Series on Risk Management, OECD Publishing, Paris, www.oecd.org/officialdocuments/publicdisplaydocumentpdf/?cote=env/jm/mono(2011)4&doclanguage=en.

OECD (2010), *Cutting Costs in Chemicals Management: How OECD Helps Governments and Industry*, OECD Publishing, Paris, https://doi.org/10.1787/9789264085930-en.

OECD (2008a), *Resolution of the Council on Implementation of the Strategic Approach to International Chemicals Management (SAICM)*, C(2008)32, OECD Publishing, Paris, www.oecd.org/dataoecd/15/5/40573587.pdf.

OECD (2008b), *OECD Environmental Outlook to 2030*, OECD Publishing, Paris, https://doi.org/10.1787/9789264040519-en.

OECD (2007), "The 2007 OECD list of high production volume chemicals", *Series on Testing and Assessment*, No. 112, ENV/JM/MONO(2009)40, OECD Publishing, Paris, www.oecd.org/officialdocuments/publicdisplaydocumentpdf/?cote=env/jm/mono(2009)40&doclanguage=en.

OECD (2001), "OECD environmental strategy for the first decade of the 21st century", OECD Publishing, Paris, www.oecd.org/environment/indicators-modelling-outlooks/1863539.pdf.

OECD (1998), *OECD Principles on Good Laboratory Practice*, OECD Series on Principles of Good Laboratory Practice and Compliance Monitoring, No. 1, OECD Publishing, Paris, https://doi.org/10.1787/9789264078536-en.

SAICM (2018), "The role of OECD in the implementation of SAICM and the sound management of chemicals and waste beyond 2020", Strategic Approach to International Chemicals Management, Geneva, www.saicm.org/Portals/12/documents/meetings/IP2/IP_2_INF_6_OECD_post2020.pdf.

UNEP (2013), *Global Chemicals Outlook: Towards Sound Management of Chemicals*, United Nations Environment Programme, https://wedocs.unep.org/bitstream/handle/20.500.11822/8455/-Global%20chemicals%20outlook_%20towards%20sound%20management%20of%20chemicals-2013Global%20Chemicals%20Outlook.pdf?amp%3BisAllowed=&sequence=3.

2. Quantifying the costs and savings of the OECD Environment, Health and Safety Programme

This chapter summarises the approach used to quantify the costs to governments and industry participating in the OECD Environment, Health and Safety Programme as well as the savings they derive from participating in the programme. It looks at the costs to the participating countries' and Secretariat costs. It then discusses the savings due to reducing duplicative testing of new and existing industrial chemicals, pesticides and biocides; using harmonised dossiers for pesticide registrations and harmonised country pesticide review reports; and reducing the number of test animals.

2.1. Background

In 2010, a report published by the OECD Environment, Health and Safety (EHS) Programme documented cost savings to governments and the chemicals and pesticide industries in OECD countries, from participating in the work of, and benefiting from the products developed by, the EHS Programme (OECD, 2010). The report, based on data from 2006-08, estimated that net savings (after deducting participation and OECD Secretariat costs) were around EUR 177 million a year,[1] not counting non-quantifiable savings and other benefits.

As the programme has evolved, new opportunities for work sharing are bringing even more benefits to society, particularly with regard to progress made on (Quantitative) Structure-Activity Relationships - or (Q)SARs - and read-across (see Box 2.2), the OECD (Q)SAR Toolbox, and other risk assessment guidance documents and formats. Ten years on since the last collection of data, it is time to reassess the programme and the benefits it offers in the light of these changes as well as to quantify additional benefits to governments and industry from EHS work on biocides, which were not evaluated in the previous report. This chapter summarises the approach used to quantify the costs to governments and industry of participating in the EHS Programme and the savings they derive from participating in the programme. Chapter 3 summarises the many and substantial non-quantifiable benefits for governments and industry of participating in the EHS Programme.

Four surveys[2] were conducted in April 2018 to collect data from OECD governments (see Table A.1 in Annex A) and the biocide, industrial chemicals and pesticide industries (see Table A.2 in Annex A). Additional data were collected from the OECD's Event Management System, which contains data on the number of OECD meetings held each day and the number of delegates registered for those meetings. Data from relevant reports in the literature have also been used to complement and confirm data collected via the surveys.

In this chapter, the costs of the EHS Programme are calculated first, followed by an assessment of the savings.[3] Costs are then subtracted from savings to reveal the net savings. The programme's costs and savings as presented in the report from 2010 (based on data from 2006-08) are compared with those in 2019 (based on data from 2016-18) at the end of each section.

2.2. Quantifying the costs of the EHS Programme

There are two main types of costs involved in implementing the EHS Programme:

1. Secretariat costs: OECD Secretariat support, including staff salaries, benefits and travel; consultants and invited experts; and general overhead.

2. Country costs: the costs to delegates of participating in and contributing to the work of the EHS Programme. These include both travel costs to attend OECD meetings and staff costs for developing and reviewing EHS documents and preparing for and attending EHS meetings.

The following baselines and calculations were used for this analysis:

- Secretariat costs were based on the OECD Programme of Work and Budget for the years 2016 and 2017.

- Country staff costs were calculated based on the number of delegates who participated in EHS meetings, the average length of those meetings, the time delegates spent preparing for the meetings and their average hourly wage. The figures used for the number of meetings, length of meetings and number of participants to those meetings were based on data collected from OECD's Event Management System and were averaged to compensate for yearly fluctuations in meeting frequencies. The average hourly wage across countries, as well as the average preparation time for the meetings (as a percentage of meeting time), were based on the results of the EHS survey of governments (see Annex A).

- Country travel costs were based on a weighted average of the costs of flights from five regions from which delegates travelled to OECD meetings during 2016 and 2017 (North America, South America, Europe, Asia/Pacific, and South and Southeast Asia). These costs also include the average daily expenses for delegates' meals and accommodation (i.e. EUR 304, based on discussions with government delegates).

2.2.1. Overall costs

Table 2.1 shows the estimated annual costs of the EHS Programme (averaged over two years). Box 2.1 compares the Secretariat costs in 2010 and 2019[4].

Table 2.1. **Estimated total annual costs of supporting the EHS Programme**

Country costs	
Number of meetings	42
Average length of meetings (days)	2.11
Average number of participants	1 239.50
Travel costs[1]	EUR 1 455 000
Country staff costs[2]	EUR 2 354 000
Total country costs	EUR 3 809 000
Secretariat costs	
Expenditure on permanent staff and consultancy funds	EUR 1 866 000
Extrabudgetary Chemicals Management Programme	EUR 2 679 000
Total Secretariat costs	EUR 4 545 000
Total costs (Secretariat + countries)	**EUR 8 354 000**

Notes:
1. Travel costs (rounded) = travel [weighted average cost of round-trip flight (EUR 532.64) x number of participants (1 239.50)] + expenses [length of meetings (2.11 days) x daily expenses (EUR 304) x number of participants (1 239.50)].
2. Country staff costs (rounded) = participation [length of meetings in hours (2.11 x 8 = 16.88) x number of participants (1 239.50) x staff costs per hour (EUR 45)] + preparation [(150% x 16.88 = 28.86) x number of participants (1 239.50) x staff costs per hour (EUR 45)].

Box 2.1. **Comparison of Secretariat and country costs, 2010 and 2019**

Total Secretariat costs have grown by 10% in real terms over the period 2010 to 2019, from EUR 4 137 814 in 2010 to EUR 4 545 000 in 2019. At the same time, there has been a substantial decline in country costs (68%) – due to a decrease in the number of meetings held each year – such that the overall cost of the EHS programme has been reduced by EUR 9 247 720 per year (50%), from EUR 17 601 720 in 2010 to EUR 8 354 000 in 2019. The reduction in the number of meetings is a result of the much wider use of conference calls rather than in-person meetings.

2.3. Quantifying the savings from the EHS Programme

There are both quantifiable and non-quantifiable benefits from the EHS Programme that accrue to government and industry. The savings associated with testing and assessing new pesticides and biocides, as well as new and existing industrial chemicals, can be relatively easily quantified in monetary terms. These are presented in Table 2.2. (Table 2.2 also quantifies the number of animals that are not needed each year for only testing new industrial chemicals, due to the work of the EHS Programme. That is, it does not include reductions in animals needed each year for testing existing industrial chemicals, biocides and pesticides.)

Other activities within the EHS Programme can currently only be described in qualitative terms, either because the benefits are not easy to measure in direct monetary gains, or else because the activities have not been implemented for a sufficient length of time to gauge their impact. However, the programme's qualitative benefits are no less real, less likely to occur or less important than the quantifiable benefits. They are listed in Chapter 3.

Table 2.2. **Annual benefits of the EHS Programme**

Savings	
From no repeat pesticide testing	EUR 206 937 500
From no repeat new industrial chemical testing	EUR 44 728 943
From no repeat biocide testing	EUR 61 250 000
From no repeat existing chemical testing	EUR 780 570
From harmonised pesticide monographs	EUR 2 218 145
From harmonised pesticide dossiers	EUR 1 951 125
Savings subtotal (rounded)	EUR 317 870 000
Costs	
Country	EUR 3 809 000
OECD Secretariat	EUR 4 545 000
Costs subtotal (rounded)	EUR 8 354 000
Net savings (rounded)	**EUR 309 516 000**
Reduction in animals needed for testing new industrial chemicals	32 702

2.3.1. Assumptions

One of the principal values of the EHS Programme is that it helps to reduce duplication of work for industry and governments. As described above, the potential for duplication is great, given the international character of biocides, industrial chemicals, and pesticide products developed for and sold in multiple markets. To calculate the extent to which OECD work helps to avoid such duplication, several assumptions were made:

- Each (often multinational) company that in a given year conducted safety testing and notified or registered a new biocide, industrial chemical or pesticide in one or more countries in one OECD region (see the paragraph below) also did this in the other regions made up of OECD member countries and the six non-members who are full adherents to OECD's MAD system (i.e. Argentina, Brazil, India, Malaysia, Singapore and South Africa).

- In this report, OECD member countries and the non-member full adherent countries to MAD are generally not considered individually, but rather as part of major regional markets. In the 2010 report, based on responses to questionnaires completed by the chemicals and pesticides industries, companies reported that, in general, they marketed their products to three OECD regions (Asia/Pacific, Europe and North America) and that because of the OECD MAD system, data generated in one region would be accepted in the two other regions. However, this does not account for savings that accrue to non-members (and their industries) that are full adherents to MAD (Argentina, Brazil, India, Malaysia, Singapore and South Africa). Further, the OECD's membership has grown from 30 member countries in 2010 to 37 today with the addition of Chile, Colombia,[5] Estonia, Israel, Latvia, Lithuania and Slovenia. Depending on the industrial sector, a conservative estimate based on the results from the latest survey (Annex B) reveals that the average number of OECD regions to which products are marketed now ranges from 3 to 3.5. (A breakdown of the countries and regions considered in this report can be found in Annex C.) Again, it was assumed that for each new product notified or registered in one region, this was also done in the other regions.

- Without the OECD MAD system, slightly different test methods and GLP principles would have been developed by each country/region independently. Based on the results of the EHS surveys of the biocides, pesticides and industrial chemical industries (see Table A.2 in Annex A), it is estimated that in the absence of the EHS Programme, Country B would not accept the following shares of biocides, pesticides and industrial chemical industries' test data emerging from Country A because of differing methods, and therefore, that testing would have to be repeated:

  o   30% of the test data for industrial chemicals

  o   35% of test data for new pesticides

  o   35% of the test data for *biocides*

  It follows from the above that approximately 65% to 70% of the data *would* be accepted in Country B, even if the data does not fully conform to the requirements of that country[6]. This shows that these are quite conservative estimates, as countries are unlikely to accept such a high share of test data that is based on a different methodology than their own.

- In the *absence* of the OECD principles and guidance, it would be less likely that a (Q)SAR/category/read-across result (Box 2.2) used in one country/region for industrial chemicals would be accepted in another country/region. The same rate of acceptance of (Q)SAR data and results from categories/read-across was assumed as for testing (i.e. 30% of (Q)SAR results developed in one country would not be accepted in another). This rate is roughly in line with the rate estimated in the 2010 report (36%).

Box 2.2. **(Quantitative) structure-activity relationships and the (Q)SAR Toolbox**

(Quantitative) structure-activity relationships, or (Q)SARs, are mathematical approaches designed to find relationships between the chemical structures (or structure-related properties) and biological activity (or target property) of the studied compounds. Convergence of use of data from these models was facilitated by the publication of the *OECD Principles for the Validation, for Regulatory Purposes, of (Q)SAR Methods* (OECD, 2004) and the OECD *Guidance on Grouping of Chemicals* (OECD, 2007, updated in 2014). Prior to the adoption of the OECD guidance, the use of (Q)SAR results or data from categories/read-across (i.e. techniques for filling data gaps within chemical categories)[1] was, in general, limited to the country which generated these results (OECD, 2006).

Since the 2010 report, the OECD has undertaken further work on (Q)SARs. The OECD (Q)SAR project works to facilitate the practical application of (Q)SAR approaches in regulatory contexts and improve their regulatory use through the development of principles for the validation of (Q)SAR models, guidance documents and the development of the OECD (Q)SAR Toolbox. Version 1 of the Toolbox was released in March 2008 and the most recent version (4.2) was released in January 2018. It has benefited from the contributions of numerous experts in governments, non-governmental organisations and the chemical industry and is designed to help registrants and authorities to, among other things, fill data gaps by read-across, trend analysis and (Q)SARs.

By providing non-testing information on toxicological and ecotoxicological endpoints, where it can be applied, the Toolbox reduces the need for laboratory experiments. In this way, both the cost of the information requirements and the number of animals used in testing is reduced for those substances.

1. The principle of the read-across technique is that endpoint or test information for one chemical is used to predict the same endpoint or test information for another chemical, which is considered to be similar by scientific justification. A chemical used to make an estimate can be referred to as a source chemical, and a chemical for which an endpoint is estimated can be referred to as a target chemical.

2.4. Reducing testing and repeat testing for new industrial chemicals

Each year, industrial chemical manufacturers notify governments of their intention to manufacture and market new substances. This notification is accompanied by a set of data to allow the safety of the chemical to be assessed. This may involve tests that range from the inexpensive (e.g. a skin irritation/corrosion study costs around EUR 2 192 – see Table B.1 in Annex B), to complicated and costly (e.g. a repeated dose toxicity study (all routes) costs around EUR 316 131). The level of information required for a new chemical assessment depends on the type of product being considered and its production volume. Analysis of data from the European Chemicals Agency (ECHA) on the actual number of new experimental studies undertaken on new substances between 2010 and 2016 (see Table B.2 in Annex B) suggests average statistical test costs of EUR 169 531 per substance.[7]

The same data set provides data on the number of new substances fulfilling data requirements using (Q)SARs/read-across. Analysis of these data suggests that the average cost saving through (Q)SARS/read-across, to a large extent supported by the OECD (Q)SAR Toolbox and guidance, is EUR 20 545 per substance. (*Note:* this ratio of statistical testing costs to (Q)SARs [90:10] is fairly close to the estimates provided from the industry survey [95:5]). This means that in the absence of the OECD (Q)SAR Toolbox and guidance, it is estimated that new substance registration would cost EUR 190 076 per substance.

Having to repeat tests for each new market can be a significant obstacle to trade in chemicals. This analysis assumes that by using OECD Test Guidelines and GLP Principles, the OECD (Q)SAR Toolbox and associated guidance, and as a result of the MAD system, a company can be assured that its test data will be accepted for assessment by governments throughout the OECD and beyond. (According to the EHS survey of the industrial chemicals sector, on average, each new chemical is introduced in three regions.) As can be seen from Table 2.3, these efforts combined continue to generate significant savings for companies whose products are introduced in multiple markets.

Table 2.3. **Benefits of the Mutual Acceptance of Data system and the (Q)SAR Toolbox: Lowering the costs of launching new industrial chemicals**

Average number of substances introduced in three major OECD regions in 2018	332.3[1]
Average cost of testing per chemical	EUR 169 531[2]
Average savings (cost avoided) through (Q)SARs/read-across per chemical	EUR 20 545[2]
Total cost of testing in the absence of (Q)SARs	EUR 190 076[2]
Average number of regions into which the new chemical is marketed	3
Total cost of testing across all regions in the absence of Mutual Acceptance of Data (MAD) and OECD (Q)SAR Toolbox and guidance[3]	EUR 101 069 745
Total cost of testing across all regions with MAD and OECD (Q)SAR Toolbox and associated guidance[4]	EUR 56 340 802
Annual savings due to the OECD Environment, Health and Safety Programme (MAD and (Q)SARs)	EUR 44 728 943
– of which through MAD[5]	EUR 39 894 265
– of which through application of (Q)SARs[6]	EUR 4 834 677

Notes:
1. Based on data from the EHS survey of governments (see Table A.1 in Annex A).
2. See Table B.2 in Annex B.
3. [Number of substances (332.3) x cost of testing without (Q)SARs (EUR 190 076)] + 2 x [percentage of tests not accepted (30%) x number of substances (332.3) x cost of testing without (Q)SARs (EUR 190 076)].
4. Number of substances (332.3) x cost of testing (169 531). This assumes there are little or no costs to generating (Q)SAR data.
5. [Testing costs (EUR 169 531) / total cost of testing in the absence of (Q)SARs (EUR 190 076)] x annual savings (EUR 44 728 943) = EUR 39 894 265.
6. [Average savings through (Q)SARs/read-across per chemical (EUR 20 545) / total cost of testing in the absence of (Q)SARs (EUR 190 076)] x annual savings (EUR 44 728 943).

In addition to the cost savings to industry through reductions in testing and repeat testing owing to MAD and the application of (Q)SARs/read-across, there is a substantial reduction in the number of test animals used to complete information requirements. The same methods used to estimate costs and cost savings above as a result of MAD and (Q)SARs/read-across can be applied to estimate the number of animals used for testing. Based on this approach, this report suggests a substantial reduction (56%) in the number of test animals that are needed (Table 2.4 and Box 2.3).

Table 2.4. **Benefits of the Mutual Acceptance of Data system
and the OECD (Q)SAR Toolbox: Reducing the number of test animals**

Average number of substances introduced in three OECD regions in 2018	332.3[1]
Average number of animals used in testing per chemical	76[2]
Average number of test animals avoided through use of (Q)SARs/read-across per chemical	33[2]
Total number of test animals that would be used in the absence of (Q)SARs per chemical	109[2]
Total number of test animals that would be used across all three regions in absence of Mutual Acceptance of Data (MAD) and the OECD (Q)SAR Toolbox and associated guidance[3]	57 959
Total number of test animals used across all three regions with MAD and (Q)SARs[4]	25 257
Annual reductions in test animals due to the OECD Environment, Health and Safety Programme (MAD and (Q)SARs)	32 702
– of which through MAD[5]	22 801
– of which through application of (Q)SARs[6]	9 901

Notes:
1. Based on data from the EHS survey of governments (see Table A.1 in Annex A).
2. See Table B.2 in Annex B.
3. [Number of substances (332.3) x test animals without (Q)SARs (109)] + 2 x [percentage of tests not accepted (30%) x number of substances (332.3) x test animals without (Q)SARs (109)].
4. Number of substances (332.3) x test animals for experimental studies (76).
5. [Average number of animals used in testing (76) / total number of animals used in absence of (Q)SARs (109)] x annual reductions in test animals due to MAD and (Q)SARs (32 702).
6. [Average number of animals avoided through (Q)SARs/read-across per chemical (33) / total number of animals used in absence of (Q)SARs (109)] x annual reductions in test animals due to MAD and (Q)SARs (32 702).

Box 2.3. **Report on significant reduction in animal testing due to the use of read-across and (Q)SARs**

Stanton and Kruszewski (2016) found that through the use of read-across and (Q)SAR techniques to fill data gaps for 261 chemical substances, 100 000 to 150 000 test animals were not needed, and USD 50 million to USD 70 million in testing costs were avoided.

2.5. Reducing repeat testing for new pesticides

According to the survey responses received from pesticide manufacturers, the average testing cost to generate the extensive data package required for a new pesticide is around EUR 21.5 million.

Having to repeat tests for each new market can be a significant obstacle to trade in pesticides. This OECD analysis assumes that by using OECD Test Guidelines and GLP Principles, and as a result of the MAD system, a company can be assured that its test data will be accepted for assessment by governments throughout the OECD and beyond, i.e. in 3.5 regions.[8] As can be seen from Table 2.5, the MAD system has therefore generated, and continues to generate, significant savings for companies whose products are introduced in multiple markets.

Table 2.5. **Mutual Acceptance of Data system benefits:**
Lowering the costs of launching new pesticides

Average number of substances introduced in each of the 3.5 major OECD regions in 2018	11[1]
Average cost of testing per chemical	EUR 21 500 000[2]
Total cost of testing across all 3.5 regions in the absence of Mutual Acceptance of Data (MAD)[3]	EUR 443 437 500
Total cost of testing across all 3.5 regions with MAD[4]	EUR 236 500 000
Annual savings due to the OECD Environment, Health and Safety Programme	EUR 206 937 500

Notes:
1. Based on data from the EHS survey of governments (see Table A.1 in Annex A).
2. Based on data from the EHS survey of industry (see Table A.2 in Annex A).
3. [Number of new pesticides per year (11) x cost of testing (EUR 21.5 million)] + 2.5 [percentage of tests that would have to be repeated without MAD (35%) x number of new pesticides (11) x cost of testing (EUR 21.5 million)].
4. Number of new pesticides per year (11) x cost of testing (EUR 21.5 million).

Box 2.4. **Comparison of testing costs, 2010 and 2019**

Net savings for pesticide manufacturers due to the use of OECD Test Guidelines/Good Laboratory Practice Principles rose from EUR 155 627 500 in 2010 to EUR 206 937 500 in 2019 (+33%). This increase is probably due to the following reasons:

- This report considers 0.5 additional regional markets.

- An increase in the cost of testing pesticide active ingredients for toxicity and environmental chemistry (investigation of the physical and metabolic breakdown of a potential product and assessment of the residues in plant, animal, soil and water systems), attributable to a rise in regulatory bodies' health and environmental safety data requirements. As a consequence, around 45 new Test Guidelines and 51 updated/corrected Test Guidelines have been published since 2008.

2.6. Harmonising industry dossiers for pesticides registration

The OECD Pesticides Programme aims to improve the efficiency of pesticide registration and re-registration and reduce the costs to industry and governments of the pesticide approval process. Given the extensive experience of governments and industry with pesticide registration and re-registration, costs could be reduced through greater co-operation among countries in sharing data and assessments.

One approach to reducing the time and effort needed for pesticide (re-)registration is to harmonise national formats for the registration dossiers used by industry to submit data. A harmonised format means that once a company compiles a dossier for one country, the cost and time involved in developing dossiers for other countries will be significantly reduced. The OECD has a standard dossier format (OECD, 2005a) which pesticide companies can use when submitting data to member countries. According to the EHS survey of the pesticides industry, the total cost of preparing a dossier on a pesticide is EUR 236 500 (not including the cost of testing). Industry has estimated that using the OECD format saves an average of 70% of the costs of developing a dossier on the same substance for a second country. In other words, using the OECD dossier format for a substance being introduced into a second country only costs a company 30% of the cost of the first dossier on the same substance. On the other hand, if the first dossier was not developed using the OECD dossier format, it is estimated to cost a company 60% of the cost of the first dossier to develop a second dossier. Based on the responses to the EHS survey of governments (see Table A.1 in Annex A), on average, 11 new pesticides enter the market each year, and each is introduced into, on average, 3.5 regional markets (meaning a company will need to prepare an average of 3.5 dossiers for each substance). Based on these assumptions, the savings to the pesticides industry from using the OECD format would therefore be EUR 1.95 million per year (Table 2.6).

It should be noted that this methodology only accounts for the savings that accrue to industry for the submission of dossiers for new active ingredients, not for the submission of dossiers for pesticide products which contain those active ingredients or for existing active ingredients which undergo periodic re-reviews but which may still use portions of the OECD dossier format.

Table 2.6. **Annual savings to industry from harmonised dossiers for pesticide registrations**

Number of new pesticides to be registered	11
Cost to prepare one dossier	EUR 236 500
Total cost to prepare dossiers for all new pesticides across all 3.5 regions without OECD harmonised dossier[1]	EUR 6 503 750
Total cost to prepare dossiers for all new pesticides across all 3.5 regions with OECD harmonised dossier[2]	EUR 4 552 625
Yearly savings due to OECD Environment, Health and Safety Programme	EUR 1 951 125

Notes:
1. (11 x EUR 236 500) + (11 x EUR 141 900) (second dossier costs 60% of the original one) x 2.5 (regions).
2. (11 x EUR 236 500) + (11 x EUR 70 950) (second dossier costs 30% of the original one) x 2.5 (regions).

Box 2.5. **Comparison of pesticide industry savings from using the OECD dossier format, 2010 and 2019**

The estimated annual savings from using the OECD dossier format has increased by 9%, from EUR 1 787 885 in 2010 to EUR 1 951 125 in 2019. Much of the additional savings are due to the consideration of 0.5 additional regional markets.

2.7. Harmonising country review reports for pesticide registration

Just as harmonising the formats used in industry registration dossiers significantly reduces costs and time for industry, harmonising the formats of country reports (monographs) which review pesticide registration submissions can also provide substantial benefits by allowing the information to be shared across governments and by allowing joint reviews of the same pesticides (see OECD, 2005b). The OECD has developed a standard monograph format[9] which governments can use to prepare their country reports.

Based on information provided in the EHS survey of governments (see Annex A), it is estimated that reviewing a full industry dossier on a new pesticide and writing a comprehensive report (monograph) takes a government 1.95 person-years. However, by using another country's monograph for the same pesticide – based on the OECD monograph format – government experts estimate that 1.02 full person-years of time would be saved (i.e. 52%), thus generating significant savings (Table 2.7). The savings in

Table 2.7 are estimated based on average staff costs per hour in OECD countries (EUR 45)[10], and 240 working days per year.

Table 2.7. **Annual savings to governments from harmonised country pesticide review reports (monographs)**

Average number of new pesticide applications each year	11
Cost to review one dossier and prepare a monograph[1]	EUR 168 480
Total cost to review dossiers and prepare monographs on all new pesticides across all 3.5 regions without OECD harmonised report format[2]	EUR 6 486 480
Total cost to review dossiers and prepare monographs on all new pesticides across all 3.5 regions with OECD harmonised report format[3]	EUR 4 268 336
Annual savings due to OECD Environment, Health and Safety Programme	EUR 2 218 145

Notes:
1. 8 hours/day x EUR 45/hour x 240 working days/year x 1.95 person-years.
2. EUR 168 480 x 11 new pesticides x 3.5 regions.
3. [EUR 168 480 x 11] + 2.5 x [52.13% (EUR 168 480 x 11)].

Box 2.6. **Comparison of government cost savings from using the OECD monograph formats, 2010 and 2019**

The savings from harmonised country review reports for pesticides in 2019 (EUR 2 218 145) represented a close to 8% decline compared to the estimated savings in 2010 (EUR 2 408 700 adjusted for inflation). This drop may have been the result of the decrease in: the average number of pesticide applications per year, from 12 in 2010 to 11 in 2019; the time needed to develop a monograph, from 2.2 to 1.95 person-years, even with the increase in the number of regions from 3 to 3.5 and the hourly cost of government staff from EUR 36 to EUR 45.

2.8. Reducing repeat testing for new biocides

The present report considers the savings for industry attributable to OECD Test Guidelines and GLP Principles for new biocidal active substances too. (These savings were not calculated in the 2010 report.) According to the survey responses received and from the literature review (Cefic Sector Groups, 2017), the average testing cost to generate the data package required for new biocidal active substances is around EUR 5 million.

As with pesticides, having to repeat tests for each new market can be a significant obstacle to trade in biocides. As a result of the MAD system, a company can be assured that its test data will be accepted for assessment by governments throughout the OECD and beyond. The MAD system therefore generates significant savings for companies that introduce biocidal products into multiple markets (Table 2.8).

Table 2.8. **MAD system benefits: Lowering the costs of launching new biocidal active substances**

Average number of biocidal active substances introduced in each of the 3.5 major OECD regions per year	14[1]
Average cost of testing per biocidal active substance	EUR 5 000 000[2]
Total cost of testing across all 3.5 regions without Mutual Acceptance of Data (MAD)	EUR 131 250 000[3]
Total cost of testing across all 3.5 regions with MAD[4]	EUR 70 000 000[4]
2019 annual savings due to the OECD Environment, Health and Safety Programme	EUR 61 250 000

Notes:
1. Based on information provided by the governments of Canada, the EU and the United States.
2. Based on data from the EHS survey of industry (see Annex A) and literature review (Cefic Sector Groups, 2017).
3. [Number of new active substances per year (14) x cost of testing (EUR 5 million)] + 2.5 x [percentage of tests that would have to be repeated without MAD (35%) x number of new active substances (14) x cost of testing (EUR 5 million)].
4. Number of new active substances per year (14) x cost of testing (EUR 5 million).

It should be noted that this methodology only accounts for the savings that accrue to industry for the submission of test data for new active ingredients, not for the submission of test data for biocidal products which contain those active ingredients or for existing active ingredients which undergo periodic re-reviews.

2.9. Reducing testing and repeat testing for existing industrial chemicals

With regards to the benefits of the EHS Programme in terms of reducing the need for new testing and repeat testing of existing industrial chemicals, the 2010 report focused on the then active High Production Volume (HPV) Chemicals Programme (see Chapter 1). Under the HPV Chemicals Programme, industry and governments collected existing information or generated new information on HPV chemicals by testing or using non-test methods like (Q)SARs or read-across to create a basic set of data (Screening Information Data Set, or SIDS) on a chemical. Based on these data, governments prepared a SIDS Initial Assessment Report (SIAR) containing the key scientific data as well as a hazard assessment and recommendations for further work. As noted in Chapter 3, with the completion of work on HPV chemicals, the EHS has established the Cooperative Chemicals Assessment Programme and continues to develop guidance and other tools to promote and support the acceptance of alternative methods, such as (Q)SARs and read-across. These tools continue to result in benefits for industry associated with the generation of data used by governments in the assessment of existing industrial chemicals.

In particular, such benefits result from OECD work in the following ways:

- the cost to industry for testing is reduced as the OECD's harmonisation of the use of predictive models (i.e. (Q)SARs/read-across) and development of the OECD (Q)SAR Toolbox reduces the need for new experimental studies to support government assessments of existing chemicals

- the cost to industry for testing is further reduced, due to MAD, if the same existing substance is assessed in more than one country (i.e. no repeat testing).

The methodology to estimate the savings from the EHS Programme is similar to that used in the evaluation of the HPV Chemicals Programme for the 2010 report, and supported by responses to the industry survey as well as analyses conducted by Risk & Policy Analysts

Limited (RPA) (see Annex B). Please note that while only a few government figures were provided in response to the survey, these confirm the order of magnitude of the data below.

Three steps were taken to calculate the savings to industry of the OECD's work:

1. Step 1: Estimate the cost of testing for one chemical by a company in one country (Country A) taking into account data that can be generated using (Q)SARs/read-across. Note: this report assumes that the cost to generate data via (Q)SAR/read-across is minimal.

2. Step 2: Compare the cost for that same company which also markets the chemical in a second country (Country B) based on how much data the government in Country B would accept from Country A: 1) with the EHS Programme (i.e. MAD and OECD work on (Q)SARs/read-across); and 2) without the EHS Programme.

3. Step 3: Calculate the savings per chemical x the annual average number of existing chemical assessments governments indicated in their survey response that they use from another country, x the average number of regions in which existing chemicals are marketed.

Step 1: When a government assesses an existing chemical, it may use three sources of data: new test data; data generated by (Q)SARs/read-across; existing data. Table 2.9 provides estimates for the percentage of data generated by testing and (Q)SARs/read-across. The cost of testing is both for actual testing and the cost of testing avoided if a company generates data via (Q)SARs/read-across. The table provides estimates using two sources: the results of the survey of the industrial chemicals sector; data compiled by the RPA, and based on data from the ECHA's *Registration Database*. As discussed in Annex B, data from the ECHA *Registration Database* has been analysed by RPA to develop a statistical cost of new experimental studies and cost avoided for (Q)SARs/read-across for substances registered in the European Union. Across all existing substances, 46% of the required endpoints were satisfied by existing data, and 54% were satisfied by new data coming from either new tests or from (Q)SARs; specifically, 21% from new testing and 33% from (Q)SARs. Using costs associated with each of the specific test endpoints, the RPA has estimated that the cost of generating all of the new data to fill gaps using full testing only (simulating a situation where (Q)SARs do not exist) would have been EUR 137 100 per substance on average. Focusing solely on the generation of data (i.e. (Q)SARs and new testing make up 100% of such data), only 61% of the required new data for registration was generated by new tests and 39% was generated using (Q)SARs.[11] The cost of the new testing is estimated as EUR 83 631 per substance. Accordingly, the savings owing to the use of (Q)SARs is EUR 53 469 per substance.

Table 2.9. **Estimated costs of testing per chemical in a single country**

		Full testing for missing endpoints	Data actually provided by:	
			(Q)SAR/read-across	New testing
Industry responses to questionnaire	Percentage of total		12.5%[3]	87.5%[3]
	Cost	EUR 152 000[2]	EUR 19 000	EUR 133 000
Risk & Policy Analysts Limited (RPA)	Percentage of total		39%[4]	61%[4]
	Cost	EUR 137 100[1]	EUR 53 469	EUR 83 631

Notes:
1. Does not account for filling gaps with existing data; estimated based on data held by the European Chemicals Agency.

2. EUR 152 000 constitutes 80% of the EUR 190 000 testing costs reported in response to the EHS Survery of Industry (i.e. it excludes existing data which make up 20% of the total). The survey of industry indicated that of the data that are generated, 10% came from (Q)SARs and 70% from new data (see Annex A).
3. 12.5% and 87.5% equate to the original responses to the EHS survey of industry responses (i.e. 10% and 70%) when excluding existing data, i.e. 20% of the total (see Annex A).
4. The figures are taken from the RPA's analysis.

Step 2: Table 2.10 compares the cost for a second country (Country B) accepting data from Country A with the EHS Programme (i.e. MAD and OECD work on (Q)SARs) and without the EHS Programme. Note: based on the results of the survey of the industrial chemicals sector, it is estimated that without MAD, Country B would not accept 30% of the test data generated in Country A (i.e. 30% would have to be repeated). Further, in the absence of the OECD principles and guidance, it would be less likely that a (Q)SAR/read-across result used in Country A would be accepted in Country B. The same rate of acceptance of (Q)SAR/read-across data was assumed as for testing (i.e. 30% of (Q)SAR industrial chemical data developed in Country A would not be accepted in Country B). This rate is relatively similar to the rate estimated in the 2010 report (36%).

Table 2.10. **Cost comparison of testing per chemical with the Environment, Health and Safety Programme and without (i.e. withoug MAD and the OECD [Q]SAR Toolbox and associated guidance)**

Country			With the EHS Programme	Without the EHS Programme	
				(% of country A's data not accepted) x (the testing costs for the remaining data)[1]	Testing costs
Industry responses	A	Cost of data generated via testing	EUR 133 000		EUR 133 000
		Cost of data generated with (Q)SARs/read-across/etc.[2]	0	0	0
	B	Cost of data generated via testing	0	30% (i.e. 30% of EUR 133 000)	EUR 39 900
		Cost of data generated with (Q)SARs/read-across/etc.[2]	0	30% (i.e. 30% of EUR 19 000)	EUR 5 700
	Total		EUR 133 000		EUR 178 600
	Savings				EUR 45 600
RPA's analysis[3]	A	Cost of data provided via testing	EUR 83 631		EUR 83 631
		Cost of data provided according to (Q)SARs/read-across/etc.[2]	0		EUR 0
	B	Cost of data provided via testing	0	30% (i.e. 30% of EUR 83 631)	EUR 25 089
		Cost of data provided according to (Q)SARs/read-across/etc.[2]	0	30% (i.e. 30% of EUR 53 469)	EUR 16 041
	Total		EUR 83 631		EUR 124 761
	Savings				EUR 41 130

Notes:
1. Data derived from Table 2.9.
2. It is assumed that the cost to provide data via (Q)SAR/read-across is minimal.
3. Estimates based on registration data from the European Chemicals Agency.

Step 3: Therefore, to determine the overall savings to industry, the savings per chemical are multiplied by the number of regions in which existing chemicals are marketed (from the EHS survey of industry), and the average yearly number of assessments one country uses from another (from the EHS survey of governments) – see Table 2.11.

Table 2.11. **Total annual savings associated with the testing of existing chemicals**

	Savings per chemical	Number of regions	Average yearly number of assessments one country uses from another	Total savings
Industry responses	EUR 45 600	3	6	EUR 820 800
Risk & Policy Analysts Limited (RPA)	EUR 41 130	3	6	EUR 740 340
Average industry and RPA				EUR 780 570

> **Box 2.7. Other longer term benefits of the Mutual Acceptance of Data system and (Q)SARs for countries that have adopted REACH-like legislation**
>
> The savings described above concern the annual benefits to industry from reduced testing of existing substances. But other one-off benefits can also be envisioned. Since the adoption of the EU REACH (Registration, Evaluation, Authorization and Restriction of Chemicals) legislation, the European Union has registered approximately 21 500 chemicals (ECHA, n.d.). Thus, registration dossiers – containing the types of test data and (Q)SAR results described above – have been prepared.
>
> Since the EU adopted REACH, other countries have developed, or are developing, similar legislation. For instance, on 1 January 2015 Korea's Act on the Registration and Evaluation of Chemicals (ARECs, or sometimes referred to as K-REACH) came into force. Similarly, on 23 December 2017 Turkey's KKDIK law came into effect with similar provisions to REACH. As a number of the substances for which REACH dossiers have been prepared would fulfil the registration requirements in other countries such as Korea and Turkey, significant one-off savings could be realised by companies who notify in the EU and these other countries, thanks, in part, to Mutual Acceptance of Data and the OECD's work on (Q)SARs.
>
> As approximately 21 500 chemicals have been registered under REACH since 2008 and a significant portion of these chemicals will also be registered in Korea and Turkey, the expected one-off savings will be orders of magnitude higher than the annual recurring savings estimated above.

Notes

1. This and all other figures in the report are adjusted for inflation and reflect 2017 currency, unless otherwise specified.

2. A fifth survey was conducted of the pharmaceutical industry; however, due to some inconsistencies in the responses, analysis of this industry has not been conducted for this report. None-the-less, Chapter 3 does include some of the information collected from the pharmaceutical industry.

3. In Tables 2.3, 2.5-2.8 and 2.10-2.11 the savings are presented without taking into account the costs of the EHS Programme (i.e. they do not reflect net savings).

4. Based on the yearly average of 2016-2017.

5. OECD countries agreed to invite Colombia to become a member of the Organisation and Colombia's membership will take effect after it has taken the appropriate steps at the national level to accede to the OECD Convention and deposited its instrument of accession with the French government, the depository of the Convention.

6. That is, for example, if an industrial chemical company conducted tests for a new product and none of those tests were conducted using OECD Test Guidelines and

GLP in an OECD or MAD adherent country, 30% of the tests would have to be repeated, while the remaining 70% would still be accepted.

7. It should be noted that, while some of the assumptions that underpin the estimate of the savings on new and existing industrial chemicals come from the analysis of REACH-generated data rather than from the EHS survey's responses, REACH data provide quite an accurate picture of the situation of the European market and, by approximation, of the other OECD markets. The costs of testing derived from the survey of the industrial chemicals sector was EUR 250 000, thus the statistical test cost used above is a conservative estimate.

8. Based on the EHS survey of industry (2018). See Annex A for details.

9. OECD Guidance for Country Data Review reports (monographs), is available at: www.oecd.org/env/ehs/pesticides-biocides/countrydatareviewreportsforagriculturalchemicalpesticides.htm.

10. Based on the EHS survey of industry (2018). See Annex A for details.

11. Based on RPA's analysis.

References

Cefic Sector Groups (2017), "Position paper: Annex I – Innovation in the biocides industry – General considerations relevant for preservatives", European Chemical Industry Council, Brussels, https://circabc.europa.eu/webdav/CircaBC/SANTE/BPR%20-%20Public/Library/CA%20meetings/70th%20CA%20meeting%20March%202017/CA-March17-Doc.5.2%20-%20Review%20of%20PT%206%20in-can%20preservatives-Industry%20position_AnnexI-Innovation.pdf.

ECHA (n.d.), "REACH registration results", webpage, European Chemicals Agency, https://echa.europa.eu/reach-registrations-since-2008 (accessed 31 August 2018).

OECD (2010), *Cutting Costs in Chemicals Management: How OECD Helps Governments and Industry*, OECD Publishing, Paris, https://doi.org/10.1787/9789264085930-en.

OECD (2007), *Guidance on Grouping of Chemicals*, OECD Series on Testing and Assessment, No. 80, OECD Publishing, Paris, https://doi.org/10.1787/9789264085831-en.

OECD (2006), "Report on the regulatory uses and applications in OECD member countries of (Quantitative) Structure-Activity Relationship [(Q)SAR] models in the assessment of new and existing chemicals", ENV/JM/MONO(2006)25, OECD Publishing, Paris, www.oecd.org/officialdocuments/publicdisplaydocumentpdf/?cote=env/jm/mono(2006)25&doclanguage=en.

OECD (2005a), "OECD guidance for industry data submissions on plant protection products and their active substances", OECD Publishing, Paris, www.oecd.org/fr/env/ess/pesticides-biocides/industrydatasubmissionsforagriculturalchemicalpesticides.htm.

OECD (2005b), "OECD guidance for country data review reports for agricultural chemical pesticides", OECD Publishing, Paris, http://www.oecd.org/env/ehs/pesticides-biocides/countrydatareviewreportsforagriculturalchemicalpesticides.htm.

OECD (2004), *Recommendation of the Council concerning Chemical Accident Prevention, Preparedness and Response*, OECD, Paris, https://legalinstruments.oecd.org/en/instruments/OECD-LEGAL-0319.

Stanton, K. and F.H. Kruszewski (2016), "Quantifying the benefits of using read-across and *in silico* techniques to fulfil hazard data requirements for chemical categories", *Regulatory Toxicology and Pharmacology*, Vol. 81, pp. 250-259, https://doi.org/10.1016/j.yrtph.2016.09.004.

3. Non-quantifiable benefits of the Environment, Health and Safety Programme

This chapter discusses the more qualitative, non-quantifiable benefits for governments and industry of participating in the OECD Environment, Health and Safety Programme. These include easier access to information on chemicals, access to harmonised templates, improved safety of manufactured nanomaterials, harmonisation of biotechnology safety assessment methods, harmonised tools to manage the risks of endocrine disrupters, reduced needs for governmental inspections of test facilities in other countries, enhanced hazard assessment methods, facilitation of the exchange of information on chemical accidents, advanced harmonisation of biocides regulation, reduced potential for repeat testing for new pharmaceuticals, and counteraction towards illegal trade of pesticides.

The previous chapter calculated the monetary savings for industry and governments as a result of the OECD's Environment, Health and Safety (EHS) Programme were calculated. This chapter discusses the more qualitative (but significant) benefits of the EHS Programme.

3.1. Facilitating access to information on chemicals

In collaboration with other key players in the area of chemicals management, the OECD has developed information systems and other tools to enhance public access to chemical hazard data and risk information prepared by government chemical review programmes.

Together with the European Chemicals Agency (ECHA), the OECD developed and maintains the eChemPortal[1] – the Global Portal to Information on Chemical Substances – in order to support regulators and industry, academics and the public in taking health and environment decisions concerning chemicals. This online portal provides direct links to multiple websites compiling information on chemical hazards, risk, exposure and use as well as chemical classifications prepared for national, regional and international chemical programmes worldwide. By facilitating access to this information, the eChemPortal helps governments achieve resource efficiencies, share the burden and avoid duplication of work across national and regional assessment programmes and, therefore, reduce animal testing.

Through the eChemPortal, governments and industry can rapidly identify publically available and relevant information (including reports, webpages and data sets) on a chemical substance, the properties and effects (for example physical properties and toxicity) of a specific substance, or substances with specific properties and effects, in addition to getting access to direct links to full data sets. The portal also contains information on chemical hazard classifications in accordance with the Globally Harmonized System of Classification and Labelling and which have undergone a review by a regulatory body or international organisation as well as information on where these classifications differ. Further, the eChemPortal provides authorities with an additional channel through which they can disseminate information from their chemical programmes widely, particularly if they have structured chemical data in, or mapped to, the OECD Harmonised Templates (see below).

3.2. Providing OECD Harmonised Templates

Writing dossiers for the electronic submission of health and safety data to regulatory authorities can be very resource-intensive. Therefore, the OECD has developed the OECD Harmonised Templates[2] for reporting information used for the risk assessment of chemicals, mainly studies conducted on chemicals to determine their properties or effects on human health and the environment, but also for storing data on use and exposure. As countries increasingly implement the OECD Harmonised Templates in their IT systems, the costs of preparing different data sets for different national/regional regulatory assessment schemes are reduced.

The OECD Harmonised Templates allow companies to gather and store their chemical test summaries in a single database and submit the same information to different authorities without having to re-enter or reformat any data. They also allow governments to easily exchange information on chemicals in a structured and harmonised format, without costly data reformatting.

3.3. Ensuring the safety of manufactured nanomaterials

The EHS Programme offers many benefits to the new and growing area of nanomaterial production and other advanced materials. These materials – which have physical, chemical and biological properties which may differ in fundamental ways from those of individual atoms and molecules – hold much promise for improving people's lives. However, the special features that make nanomaterials so useful may also pose risks to human health and/or the environment. Thus, their risks need to be properly assessed. But given the innovative structure of nanomaterials, the traditional testing and assessment methods for conventional chemicals may not always be appropriate.

OECD countries began working together to share knowledge and expertise when the use of manufactured nanomaterials was emerging as a possible concern. By co-operating on this issue before governments had fully developed programmes in response, the EHS Programme was able to ensure that the approaches for hazard, exposure and risk assessment for manufactured nanomaterials were internationally harmonised, science-based and of high quality.

The OECD's EHS Programme ensures cost savings to governments and industry in the area of safety of nanomaterials in several ways. Among others, under the Testing Programme of Manufactured Nanomaterials, OECD member countries, along with some non-member economies and other stakeholders, pooled their expertise and organised the safety testing of specific manufactured nanomaterials, seeking to identify the need for developing new Test Guidelines or adapting existing Test Guidelines to nanomaterials.

In 2013, the OECD adopted a *Recommendation of the Council on the Safety Testing and Assessment of Manufactured Nanomaterials* (OECD, 2013). An important consequence of this Recommendation is that much of the data collected as part of the safety assessment of nanomaterials will fall within the scope of the OECD Mutual Acceptance of Data (MAD) system. With OECD guidance increasingly being adapted to nanomaterials, this implies that savings similar to those generated for traditional chemicals due to MAD (as outlined in Chapter 2) eventually will also apply to nanomaterials.

The EHS Programme has developed new test methods for manufactured nanomaterials (or adapted existing methods) so that no individual government will have the burden of developing these new methods. The OECD adopted the first Test Guidelines developed specifically for nanomaterials in 2017.[3] Testing using the guidelines adopted by the OECD will fall under the MAD system and hence eliminate any duplicative testing costs.

3.4. Harmonising biotechnology safety assessments

Modern biotechnology is becoming increasingly important for agriculture, livestock farming, fisheries, forestry, industrial production and public health. Every year, more and more species are modified for various traits, including resistance to biotic and abiotic stresses, tolerance to herbicides/insecticides, and improved nutritional content for crops. Each new host organism (plants, animals and micro-organisms) and trait combination developed by a company is a new product. In the absence of an internationally harmonised approach for commercial approvals, each company must obtain approval for its engineered products in every country in which it expects to market them for production and/or use in foods or feeds. As with industrial chemicals and pesticides, the cost to industry to prepare dossiers, and to governments to review each application, can be substantial.

A considerable portion of the cost of product approval involves environmental risk (biosafety) assessments. These examine three aspects of the product: 1) its biology; 2) the specific trait introduced (e.g. virus resistance); 3) the potential impact on the environment in which it is intended to be released. Since the environmental information required is largely the same in every country, national authorities and experts involved in the EHS Programme develop "consensus documents"[4] that contain common technical elements for use during the regulatory assessment of products of modern biotechnology. Similarly for novel foods and feeds derived from these products, consensus documents are elaborated for each bioengineered crop species to provide information on compositional and nutritional parameters that are critical in comparative safety assessments.

To date, these OECD consensus documents constitute official reference tools in risk/safety assessment of the regulatory systems of many economies worldwide. Their use can contribute to mutual recognition of assessments among countries, therefore facilitating the international trade of the products. There is a reported case where the competent authority of a non-OECD country, Viet Nam – which participates as an observer in the EHS Programme – accepts the food/feed safety approvals issued by other participating authorities for granting its own national approvals for food/feed use without requiring additional tests, therefore drastically reducing the safety assessment cost. Further, the Argentinian regulation on the commercialisation of genetically modified organisms, issued in 2018, explicitly lists the situations of low level presence of transgenic grains in bulk commodities where the OECD related guidelines should be taken into account (Government of Argentina, 2018). This allows for savings in the safety assessment process by providing internationally recognised approaches to information sharing on the transgenic plant unauthorised in the importing country, with guidance on how to establish a risk profile for environmental safety, and proposing potential ways to proactively address the low level presence situation.

Hundreds of genetically engineered crop varieties and other organisms are currently in the development pipeline, each requiring a separate notification or authorisation in each country. The *BioTrack Product Database*,[5] developed by the EHS, collates information on these varieties approved for cultivation and for use in foods and feeds in OECD countries and other economies associated with the work. With the increasing commercialisation potential for these products, the use of OECD consensus documents and database information leads to significant savings for government and industry and also accelerate the assessment of these products.

In addition, the EHS Programme facilitates cross-country discussions on solutions to common emerging issues, such as new plant breeding techniques (e.g. genome editing), which in turn will reduce the possibility of differences in regulatory responses across countries. The programme ensures regular information sharing on these techniques, including through workshops such as the Conference on Genome Editing Applications in Agriculture held in June 2018.[6]

3.5. Providing harmonised tools to identify endocrine disrupters

Over the last two decades, the OECD has emerged as a key player associated with the issue of endocrine disrupters testing and assessment. In 1996, the OECD set up an Advisory Group on Endocrine Disrupters Testing and Assessment to develop new and update existing OECD Test Guidelines to identify chemicals with endocrine disrupting properties. The Advisory Group has overseen the validation of about 35 OECD Test Guidelines with endpoints that are specific for endocrine disrupters, including a variety of *in vitro* Test Guidelines that provide information on endocrine modes of action. One of the most important outcomes of the Advisory Group's work was the 2012 publication of *Guidance Document 150* (GD 150) (OECD, 2012), which was the first comprehensive, international guide for identifying endocrine disrupting chemicals. GD 150 provides guidance for analysing test results, evidence for a chemical mode of action, support for regulatory authorities' decisions on whether a substance is an endocrine disrupter, and, in some cases, recommendations for follow-up testing if a conclusion cannot be made. GD 150 also includes a conceptual framework for organising OECD Test Guidelines and other standardised test methods into levels of increasing biological complexity and may help evaluations of endocrine disrupters. The OECD updated both GD 150 and the conceptual framework in September 2018 (OECD, 2018b).

The OECD's validated methodologies on screening and testing chemicals for their endocrine disrupting potential allow governments to implement policies for assessing and managing the risk of potential endocrine disrupters, using internationally harmonised tools. Table 3.1 lists the United States Environmental Protection Agency's (US EPA) estimates of the cost of Tier 1 and Tier 2 assays carried out as part of its Endocrine Disruptor Screening Program. Those indicated in bold in the table are OECD Test Guidelines. (The table does not include estimates for Test Guidelines 407, 408, 414 and 421/422 as the United States requires these for other types of testing and they are thus not included in endocrine screening costs.)

Table 3.1. **Estimated costs of US EPA Endocrine Disruptor Screening Program Tier 1 and Tier 2 Assays**

	Estimated cost/assay (USD)
Tier 1 *in vitro* assays[1]	
OECD TG 458/OCSPP 890.1150 – Androgen Receptor Binding (Rat Prostate)*	27 700
OCSPP 890.1200 – Aromatase (Human Recombinant)	34 700
OECD TG 493/OCSPP 890.1250 – Estrogen Receptor Binding	27 100
OECD TG 455/OCSPP 890.1300 – Estrogen Receptor Transcriptional Activation (Human Cell Line HeLa-9903)	27 800
OECD TG 456/OCSPP 890.1550 – Steroidogenesis (Human Cell Line – H295R)	20 300
Total	137 600
Tier 1 *in vivo* assays[2]	
OECD TG 231/OCSPP 890.1100 – Amphibian Metamorphosis (Frog)	145 000-187 000
OECD TG 230/OCSPP 890.1350 – Fish Short-Term Reproduction	197 000-203 000
OECD TG 441/OCSPP 890.1400 – Hershberger (Rat)	154 000-192 000
OCSPP 890.1450 – Female Pubertal (Rat)	228 000-250 000
OCSPP 890.1500 – Male Pubertal (Rat)	234 000-261 000
OECD TG 440/OCSPP 890.1600 – Uterotrophic (Rat)	139 000-150 000
Total	1 152 000-1 188 000
Total cost range for US EPA Tier 1 battery	1 289 600-1 325 600
Tier 2 *in vivo* assays[2]	
OCSPP 890.2100 – Avian Two-Generation Toxicity Test in the Japanese Quail (JQTT)	473 000-643 000
OECD TG 240/OCSPP 890.2200 – Medaka Extended One-Generation Reproduction Test (MEOGRT)	488 000-669 000
OECD TG 241/OCSPP 890.2300 – Larval Amphibian Growth and Development Assay (LAGDA)	227 000-438 000
OECD TG 443 – Extended One-Generation Reproduction Toxicity Test (EOGRT) (Rat). (*Note:* May be substituted for Two-Generation Reproduction Toxicity Test in Rat, OCSPP 870.3800.)	1 274 000-1 600 000
Total cost range for US EPA Tier 2 tests	2 462 000-3 350 000

Notes: OECD Test Guidelines are highlighted in bold. Estimated costs include, but are not limited to, chemical purchase, sampling and shipment, analytical method development and measurements, range-finding assay, in-life assay, histopathology, biochemical analyses, statistical assessment, quality assurance, project management, paperwork (e.g. reports), and clerical costs.
1. Figures are from 2012 and from US EPA (2013), adjusted to 2018 USD using the US Department of Labor inflation calculator.
2. Estimates provided by the US EPA, based on the range of contract offers submitted to the US EPA in April 2015.

Other countries are setting up endocrine disrupting chemicals programmes requesting testing according to OECD Test Guidelines. One example is the European Union's endocrine disrupting chemicals criteria for pesticides and biocides, adopted in 2018 (European Commission, 2018). As more countries set up their programmes using results from OECD Test Guidelines, the potential for savings will increase. That is, as many countries will be requesting and using the same new OECD Test Guidelines the cost of testing will be less than it might otherwise have been if governments developed and used different tests developed outside of the OECD (i.e. without MAD).

3.6. Reducing the need for governmental inspections of test facilities in other countries

The OECD MAD system not only reduces duplicative testing and allows governments to share data, it also eliminates the need for governments to inspect test facilities outside their country. In the past, if a government that relied on critical health and safety test data generated in another country had concerns about the quality of that data, it needed to travel to the other country to conduct an inspection of the test facility that produced the data or conduct a study audit to verify the quality of the data. However, with the adoption of the 1989 *Decision-Recommendation of the Council on Compliance with the Principles of Good Laboratory Practice* (OECD, 1989) – which is one of the three Council acts[7] related to MAD – countries adhering to MAD can request another country to conduct an inspection of a test facility or a study audit for test facilities located in the other country. This has significantly reduced the cost of travel for the requesting country.

3.7. Enhancing hazard assessment methods

Current regulatory toxicity testing and assessment approaches largely remain based on a checklist of *in vivo* tests, conducted in accordance with standardised test guidelines or protocols such as the OECD Test Guidelines. While this approach has evolved over the past half century, it is unlikely to meet, in an efficient manner, legislative mandates that require increased numbers of chemical assessments to be undertaken without a concomitant increase in the use of animals and resources. New approaches are necessary to close the gap between the number of chemicals in use and the number assessed to date.

The OECD Cooperative Chemicals Assessment Programme, which originally was established based on the previous High Production Volume (HPV) chemicals work, was revised in 2014 to better respond to the changing needs of member countries. It addresses a number of member country challenges, such as: assessing more chemicals in a shorter period of time; addressing all chemicals on the market; and avoiding duplication of ongoing work in other countries. Recently, such work has focused on enhancing the development and application of Integrated Approaches to Testing and Assessment (IATA). IATAs are pragmatic, science-based approaches for chemical hazard characterisation that rely on an integrated analysis of existing information coupled with the generation of new information using testing strategies. IATAs can include a combination of methods and can be informed by integrating results from one or many methodological approaches, such as (Quantitative) Structure-Activity Relationship, i.e. (Q)SARs, read-across, *in vitro*, *ex vivo*, *in vivo* or omic technologies (e.g. toxicogenomics). (See further information on the OECD's work on "omics" technologies in Section 5.8.) Read-across and similar approaches can fill data for requirements for chemical categories as well as eliminate the need for many animal tests (Stanton and Kruszewski, 2016).

The EHS Programme also supports the development of Adverse Outcome Pathways (AOPs), which helps harmonise IATAs. AOPs are tools that involve capturing the underlying biology of how chemicals interact with organisms to cause adverse effects in a practical, modular format. AOPs provide decision makers with enhanced scientific understanding and greater confidence, and can thus enable the increased integration and acceptance of read-across, new approach methods and the use of *in vitro* assays.

As discussed in Chapter 2, the EHS Programme has developed, and continues to develop, guidance documents and tools for the use of alternative methods such as (Q)SARs and grouping of chemicals. The goal is that over time these new approach methodologies will not only provide a more mechanistically informed process for chemical assessment, but will also reduce the cost of testing and the need for tests on animals. In addition, moving to more harmonised approaches for hazard assessment and their technological convergence will allow countries to more readily draw upon other countries' assessments of chemicals, reducing duplication of effort.

The *Decision-Recommendation of the Council on the Co-operative Investigation and Risk Reduction of Chemicals* (OECD, 2018a), developed through the EHS Programme, was adopted on 25 May 2018 by the OECD Council. The Decision-Recommendation (which is an updated version of a 1991 Decision-Recommendation) promotes collaboration between adherents in the development of harmonised hazard and exposure assessment methodologies, and facilitates information dissemination and the sharing of the burden associated with information generation. Such collaboration will improve the quality of assessments, and reduce the time and effort required to conduct them.

3.8. Facilitating the exchange of information on chemical accidents to support prevention, preparedness and response

The potential for major industrial accidents has increased with the expansion of production, storage and use of hazardous substances. Over the past decades, such accidents have caused deaths, numerous injuries, significant environmental pollution and massive economic losses, highlighting the need for a systematic approach to the control of hazardous substances. There are also hundreds of small-scale, but recurrent, chemical accidents every year that cause severe harm to workers, communities, municipalities, businesses and the environment. In order to gauge the number and scale of accidents globally over one year, the European Commission's Joint Research Centre examined the number of accidents reported in the media from 1 October 2016 to 30 September 2017 (Wood, 2017). The study identified 667 accidents. The great majority of these occurred at fixed facilities (454) and a smaller number during transport (147), followed by pipelines (37) and offshore (9). According to the study, OECD countries accounted for nearly two-thirds of the events (421 out of 667), but barely one-third of the deaths (201 out of 579).[8]

The EHS' Chemical Accidents Programme ensures cost savings across countries by avoiding duplication of efforts to identify adequate methods for prevention, preparedness and response, and thus by reducing economic losses caused by chemical accidents. The programme has developed some of the EHS Programme's most widely used documents; the *OECD Guiding Principles for Chemical Accident Prevention, Preparedness and Response* is one example (OECD, 2003), which provides general and specific guidance for the safe planning, construction, management, operation and review of the safety performance of hazardous installations. The Guiding Principles form the basis of the 2004 *Recommendation of the Council concerning Chemical Accident Prevention, Preparedness and Response* (OECD, 2004) and are accompanied by the OECD *Guidance on Developing*

Safety Performance Indicators Related to Chemical Accident Prevention, Preparedness and Response (OECD, 2008).

3.9. Advancing harmonisation of biocides regulation

Since its establishment in 2003, the OECD Biocide Programme has sought to ensure a high level of protection for users, the public at large and the environment, and to remove non-tariff barriers to trade in biocides.[9] The programme provides a global platform for making progress in regulating, registering and placing biocidal products on the market, as well as for the exchange of best practices on the sustainable use of biocides, offering benefits to regulators as well as to industry.

Notably, the programme yields benefits to governmental authorities related to the risk assessment and evaluation of biocide products and their active substances. Harmonising essential parts of authorisation procedures enables governments to assess the risks of biocides in a quicker, more thorough and harmonised manner. The workload of countries is greatly reduced by agreeing on common evaluation methodologies and by sharing the burden of evaluation. The Biocides Programme facilitates the exchange of study evaluations between authorities, through, among other things, a new initiative known as Review Sharing of Acute Studies (see Box 1.2). This reduces the resources needed for evaluating dossiers.

As there are a wide variety of applications for biocides, estimating potential releases of these products can be very complex. As a result, the OECD has developed a number of Emission Scenario Documents (ESDs) on biocides, including on insecticides, anti-fouling products and wood preservatives. This not only reduces the need for any one government to develop such ESDs independently, it also promotes the harmonisation of release estimations across regulatory agencies. Further, the OECD has developed test methods specifically aimed at biocides (on release estimations for treated wood, efficacy for disinfectants, storage stability, insecticides and treated articles), as well as harmonised templates to report tests in a structured format. These and other OECD harmonised data and test method requirements create direct benefits for industry, by avoiding the duplication of testing in the various countries in which they operate and hence reducing the costs of testing.

3.10. Reducing repeat testing for new pharmaceuticals

Similar to companies from the industries surveyed for this report, pharmaceutical companies also conduct a number of non-clinical tests using OECD Test Guidelines and following the OECD Good Laboratory Practice Principles. Hence, significant potential benefits could accrue to this industry as a result of the MAD system. In 2016, the average number of new pharmaceutical active ingredients registered by OECD governments was 34,[10] and the cost of non-clinical testing of such substances is likely to be several million euros. Assuming that pharmaceutical companies market their products in as many regions as biocides, pesticides and industrial chemicals companies do, the savings to governments and industry resulting from the reduction in duplicative testing, due to MAD, would be substantial.

3.11. Counteracting the illegal trade of pesticides

In order to ensure food security and safety while protecting human health and the environment, the pesticides market is highly regulated. Pesticide producers face large expenses due to long-term research and development efforts, significant testing, regulatory approval and other associated development costs for new products. Production costs of pesticides are, however, relatively low. This creates opportunities for illegal traders wishing to benefit from inserting cheaper, untested and thus possibly dangerous, illegal products onto the market. In some countries, the share of illegal pesticides on the regular market is reportedly as high as 20%. Over the period 2009-14, direct and knock-on economic effects from illegal pesticides sales amounted to EUR 2.8 billion annually in the European Union alone, as a result of lost sales, subsequent employment loss and loss of government revenues (EUIPO, 2017). This is on top of the costs due to crop loss and impacts on human health and the environment caused by the use of illegal pesticides.

Since 2010, the OECD has been co-ordinating activities to counteract the illegal trade of pesticides, so that:

* countries and consumers can rely on the risk assessment and risk management policies that are in place to protect human health and the environment, and that markets are not impacted by illegal pesticides

* efforts and investments by pesticide producers when registering pesticides are not undermined by rogue traders.

For instance, the OECD has developed a Rapid Alert System, which allows regulatory authorities in OECD countries and other invited countries to rapidly exchange information on suspicious or rejected shipments of pesticides via a protected website, thereby reducing the risk of illegal pesticides entering a market. This enables countries to prevent possible damages to crops, human health and the environment resulting from the use of illegal pesticides.

Within the OECD Network on Illegal Trade of Pesticides, member countries exchange experiences and best practices in the identification of illegal pesticides and methodologies to counteract them. This has resulted in the development of a Best Practice Guidance publication (OECD, 2018c) and a draft OECD Council Recommendation for identifying and tackling illegal pesticides throughout the complete lifecycle of a pesticide (i.e. from manufacture through formulation, trade and use to final disposal). It is anticipated that the Recommendation will be adopted in early 2019. The OECD Network on Illegal Trade of Pesticides also exchanges information with the United Nations Interregional Crime and Justice Research Institute, EUROPOL, the World Customs Organisation, INTERPOL, industry and various other organisations, and informs the Strategic Approach to International Chemicals Management on a regular basis to create better policies against the illegal trade in pesticides.

Notes

1. eChemPortal, available at: www.oecd.org/env/ehs/risk-assessment/echemportalglobalportaltoinformationonchemicalsubstances.htm.

2. See: www.oecd.org/ehs/templates.

3. Test Guideline 318: Dispersion Stability of Nanomaterials in Simulated Environmental Media; Test Guideline 412: 28-Day (Subacute) Inhalation Toxicity Study; and Test Guideline 413: 90-Day (Subchronic) Inhalation Toxicity Study.

4. See the OECD webpage on the Series on "Harmonisation of Regulatory Oversight in Biotechnology": https://doi.org/10.1787/23114622.

5. *OECD BioTrack Product Database* available at: https://biotrackproductdatabase.oecd.org.

6. See: www.oecd.org/environment/genome-editing-agriculture.

7. See the OECD webpage on the "OECD Council Acts Related to the Mutual Acceptance of Data (MAD)": www.oecd.org/chemicalsafety/testing/council-acts-on-mutual-acceptance-of-data.htm.

8. It is noted that media reports do not represent all incidents that occur, since many events are not reported in (mainly EU) languages used for searching and some are not reported at all. The data generally over-represent English-speaking sources, countries with strong media sectors and those that have a strong awareness of chemical hazards.

9. "Biocides" are a diverse group of products including disinfectants used in homes and hospitals; products to preserve wood; products to prevent fouling on boats; and products to control insects, mice or rats in homes and industries.

10. Thirty-four is the average of the number of registrations of new active substances noted in the European Medical Agency's *Human Medicines Highlights* for 2015, 2016 and 2017. See: www.ema.europa.eu/ema/index.jsp?curl=pages/news_and_events/document_listing/document_listing_000256.jsp&mid=WC0b01ac0580099fbb). The same figure can be found in CIRS (2017).

References

CIRS (2017), "New drug approvals in six major authorities – 2007-2016: Focus on the internationalisation of medicines", *R&D Briefing*, No. 65, Centre for Innovation in Regulatory Science, London, www.cirsci.org/wp-content/uploads/2017/11/CIRS-RD-Briefing-65-20112017.pdf.

EUIPO (2017), "The economic cost of IPR infringement in the pesticides sector", EU Intellectual Property Office, Alicante, Spain, https://euipo.europa.eu/tunnel-web/secure/webdav/guest/document_library/observatory/resources/research-and-studies/ip_infringement/study10/pesticides_sector_en.pdf.

European Commission (2018), "Commission Regulation (EU) 2018/605 of 19 April 2018 amending Annex II to Regulation (EC) No. 1107/2009 by setting out scientific criteria for the determination of endocrine disrupting properties", *Official Journal of the European Union*, L101/33-36, Publications

Office of the European Union, Brussels, https://eur-lex.europa.eu/legal-content/EN/TXT/?uri=CELEX%3A32018R0605.

Government of Argentina (2018), *Resolución 26/2018: Procedimiento de Autorización Comercial a los Organismos Genéticamente Modificados (OGM)*, Buenos Aires, *https://www.erreius.com/Legislacion/documento/20180518075705968*.

OECD (2018a), *Decision-Recommendation of the Council on the Co-operative Investigation and Risk Reduction of Chemicals*, OECD, Paris, https://legalinstruments.oecd.org/en/instruments/OECD-LEGAL-0441.

OECD (2018b), *Revised Guidance Document 150 on Standardised Test Guidelines for Evaluating Chemicals for Endocrine Disruption*, OECD Series on Testing and Assessment, No. 150, OECD Publishing, Paris, https://doi.org/10.1787/9789264304741-en.

OECD (2018c), "Best Practice Guide to Identify Illegal Trade of Pesticides", *Series on Pesticides*, No. 99, ENV/JM/MONO(2018)35, OECD Publishing, Paris, www.oecd.org/officialdocuments/publicdisplaydocumentpdf/?cote=env/jm/mono(2018)35&doclanguage=en.

OECD (2013), *Recommendation of the Council on the Safety Testing and Assessment of Manufactured Nanomaterials*, OECD, Paris, https://legalinstruments.oecd.org/en/instruments/298.

OECD (2012), "Guidance document on standardised test guidelines for evaluating chemicals for endocrine disruption", *Series on Testing and Assessment*, No. 150, ENV/JM/MONO(2012)22, OECD Publishing, Paris, www.oecd.org/officialdocuments/publicdisplaydocumentpdf/?cote=env/jm/mono(2012)22&doclanguage=en.

OECD (2008), *Guidance on Developing Safety Performance Indicators Related to Chemical Accident Prevention, Preparedness and Response,* OECD, Paris, www.oecd-ilibrary.org/environment/guidance-on-developing-safety-performance-indicators-for-public-authorities-and-communities-public_9789264221734-en;jsessionid=YbEFm-nVFFQcna_qyc-5JhJw.ip-10-240-5-76.

OECD (2004), "OECD principles for the validation, for regulatory purposes, of (Quantitative) Structure-Activity Relationship Models", http://www.oecd.org/env/ehs/risk-assessment/37849783.pdf

OECD (2003), *OECD Guiding Principles for Chemical Accident Prevention, Preparedness and Response: Guidance for Industry (Including management and Labour), Public Authorities, Communities and Other Stakeholders*, OECD, Paris, www.oecd.org/env/ehs/chemical-accidents/Guiding-principles-chemical-accident.pdf.

OECD (1989), *Decision-Recommendation of the Council on Compliance with Principles of Good Laboratory Practice*, OECD/LEGAL/0252, OECD, Paris, https://legalinstruments.oecd.org/en/instruments/58.

Stanton, K. and F.H. Kruszewski (2016), "Quantifying the benefits of using read-across and in silico techniques to fulfil hazard data requirements for chemical categories", *Regulatory Toxicology and Pharmacology*, Vol. 81, pp. 250-259, https://doi.org/10.1016/j.yrtph.2016.09.004.

US EPA (2013), "Attachment F: Calculations for paperwork burden and costs for data generation activities (as of April 3, 2013)", EDSP ICR Addendum (EDSP ICR Addendum, Attachment F. EPA ICR #2488.01; OMB # 2070-[new]), United States Environmental Protection Agency, Washington, DC, https://www.regulations.gov/document?D=EPA-HQ-OPPT-2013-0275-0017.

Wood, M. (2017), "Incidents in the media – 1 October 2016 to 30 September 2017", European Commission Joint Research Centre, presentation to the 2017 Annual Meeting of the OECD Working Group on Chemical Accidents.

4. Conclusions

This report estimated the net annual savings that accrue to governments and industry in OECD countries and non-member countries which adhere to the OECD system of Mutual Acceptance of Data (MAD), as a result of the work of the Environment, Health and Safety (EHS) Programme. These net savings were derived by quantifying the overall benefits (where possible) and subtracting the costs of the EHS Programme.

The programme costs to OECD governments total EUR 8.8 million a year.[1] These costs include the costs of experts to prepare for and attend meetings and to review and write documents as well as government funding of the OECD EHS Secretariat.

The net savings brought by the programme (i.e. after deducting costs) for harmonising the testing and assessment of new biocides, new and existing industrial chemicals, and pesticides, are estimated to be more than EUR 309 million a year (Table 4.1).

Table 4.1. **Estimated annual costs and savings of the OECD's Environment, Health and Saftey (EHS) Programme**

Costs to government of participating in the EHS Programme		Savings for governments and industry resulting from the EHS Programme	
Organisation	Cost (EUR)	Activity (chemical)	Savings (EUR)
Governments	3 809 000	From no repeat testing (pesticides) (see Table 2.5)	206 937 500
		From harmonised monographs (pesticides) (see Table 2.7)	2 218 145
		From harmonised dossiers (pesticides) (see Table 2.6)	1 951 125
		From no repeat testing (biocides) (see Table 2.8)	61 250 000
Secretariat	4 545 000	From no repeat testing (new industrial chemicals) (see Table 2.3)	44 728 943
		From no repeat testing (existing industrial chemicals) (see Table 2.11)	780 570
Total (rounded)	8 354 000 (see Table 2.1)	Total (rounded)	317 870 000
Net savings due to the EHS Proramme = EUR 309 516 000 (rounded)			

This report estimates that <u>net</u> savings[2] attributable to the EHS Programme have grown by 75% since the last report and by over 240% since the initial report (Figure 4.1 shows the absolute growth). However, it is important to note that, unlike for the previous two reports, this report includes an estimate of the significant savings from tests on biocides not being repeated due to MAD. In addition, since the last report, there has been an increase in the number of OECD member countries and non-member full adherents to MAD. This means that the reduction in duplicative testing is now spread across more countries and hence the savings are greater.

Figure 4.1. **Annual net savings to governments and industry from the Environment, Health and Safety (EHS) Programme**

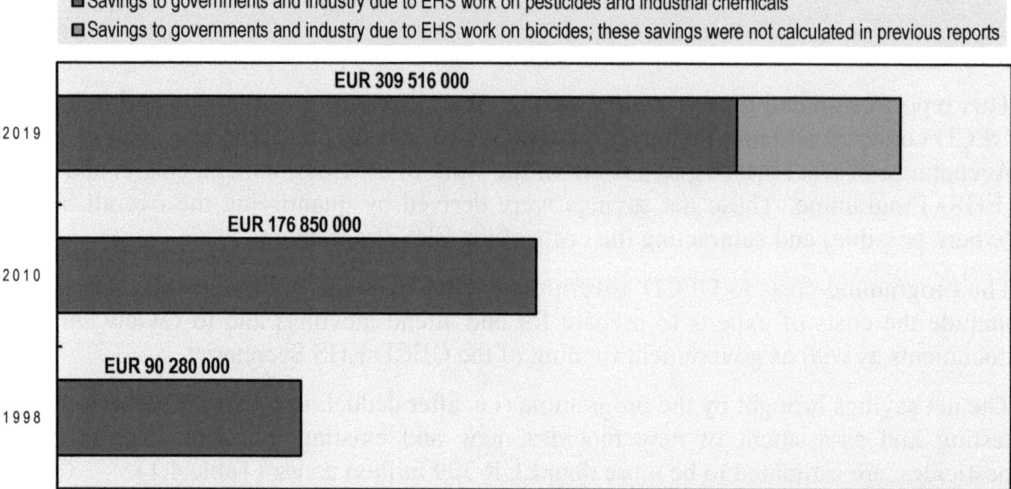

Notes:
Figures have been adjusted for inflation.

Such savings are not just monetary in nature. By reducing the need for duplicative testing of chemicals due to the OECD MAD system, almost 33 000 less animals are needed every year to test new industrial chemicals. While not quantified in this report, due to the much greater amount of testing needed for biocides and pesticides, it is expected that an even more significant number of animals will not need to be sacrificed to assess the safety of these chemicals.

In developing this report, it was not possible to quantify all of the benefits of the EHS Programme's work. However, these unquantified benefits are just as real, likely and important as the quantified benefits (see Chapter 3). Some examples of work which leads (or will lead) to non-quantified benefits for governments and industry are:

- ensuring safer nanomaterials by developing harmonised tools for testing and assessment

- harmonising the safety assessment methodologies for products of modern biotechnology

- providing harmonised tools to identify the risks of endocrine disrupters

- reducing the need for national government inspections of test facilities in other countries which test chemicals

- enhancing hazard assessment methods and limiting the use of animals in chemical testing

- facilitating the exchange of information on chemical accidents to support prevention, preparedness and response

- advancing harmonisation of biocides regulations and testing

- reducing repeat testing for new pharmaceuticals

- counteracting the illegal trade of pesticides and thus reducing the chance that unregulated, unsafe and ineffective products are used on crops.

Also excluded are the benefits to industry of avoiding delays in marketing new products. According to industry sources, these could represent similar amounts to those saved by avoiding duplicative testing (for example, delays in the registration of a pesticide might lead to missed sales for a full growing season). Also excluded are the added benefits to health and the environment of governments working together to be able to evaluate and manage more chemicals than they would if they worked independently. Finally, while pharmaceuticals were not the subject of this analysis, it is expected that due to the extensive non-clinical testing required for such products, and because many of these test methods may fall within the MAD system, the benefits of the EHS Programme for these products could be extensive.

With more than 40 years of experience and a vast area of work, the EHS Programme ensures safer and more efficient chemicals policies and promotes more sustainable development in OECD member countries and key partner countries around the world. This report has demonstrated that the programmes' benefits to society amount to more than EUR 309 million and tens of thousands of animal lives saved every year, in addition to numerous non-quantifiable benefits. With the more recent parts of the EHS Programme evolving and better methodologies being developed, many of the qualitative benefits may be quantifiable in the future.

Notes

1. These costs are significantly lower than the cost estimates in the 2010 report – EUR 15.2 million a year – due in large part to a significant increase in the use of conference calls in lieu of face-to-face meetings.

2. Due to some minor differences in data and methodologies, the comparison between the 1998 and 2010 savings is an approximation.

Annex A. Responses from the survey of governments and industry

Table A.1. **Government responses to the 2018 Environment, Health an Safety Survey**
(average values)

Average hourly cost of staff	EUR 45
Time to prepare for an OECD meeting as a percentage of meeting time	150%
Average number of new industrial chemicals notified each year	332.3
Average number of assessments of existing industrial chemicals per year	13
For how many of those assessments is an existing assessment from another OECD country available?	5
Average staff time spent to develop one assessment report on a new or existing industrial chemical (hours)	457
Percentage of staff time that would be reduced if an assessment for the same chemical from another OECD country exists	35%
What percentage of this is due to the other country using OECD guidance and formats?	35%
Average number of pesticide applications for active ingredients received per year	11
Average number of biocide applications for active ingredients received per year	14
Average number of person-years to review a pesticide dossier and prepare a monograph	1.95
Per cent less time if country already had a full pesticide monograph provided by another country rather than preparing the initial pesticide monograph	52%

Table A.2. **Industry responses to the 2018 Environment, Health an Safety Survey**
(average values)

Cost of base set testing for a new industrial chemical	EUR 250 000
Cost of base set testing for an existing industrial chemical	EUR 190 000
Percentage of endpoint data for industrial chemicals fulfilled by new testing	70%
Percentage of endpoint data for industrial chemicals fulfilled by (Q)SARs [(quantitative) structure-activity relationships]	10%
Percentage of endpoint data for industrial chemicals fulfilled by existing data	20%
Cost of testing for a new biocide – active substance	EUR 5 000 000
Cost of testing for a new pesticide – active substance	EUR 21 500 000
Per cent of industrial chemical testing that would have to be repeated without OECD Test Guidelines, Good Laboratory Practice (GLP) Principles and the MAD system	30%
Per cent of pesticide testing that would have to be repeated without OECD Test Guidelines, GLP Principles and the MAD system	35%
Per cent of biocide testing that would have to be repeated without OECD Test Guidelines, GLP Principles and the MAD system	35%
Average number of markets in which industrial chemicals are marketed	3
Average number of markets in which pesticides are marketed	3.5
Average number of markets in which biocides are marketed	3.5
Average cost to prepare a pesticide dossier	EUR 236 500
Per cent of cost of preparing a first dossier that would be needed for a second dossier if the first was prepared in the OECD format	30%
Per cent of cost of preparing a first dossier that would be needed for a second dossier if the first was not prepared in the OECD format	70%

Annex B. RPA analysis of the cost of testing and (Q)SARs based on data from the European Chemicals Agency's *Registration Database*

The European Chemicals Agency (ECHA) has undertaken analyses of new substances and existing substances registered under the REACH Regulation in the European Union to determine the extent to which the following have been used to fulfil information requirements for each (eco)toxicological endpoint:

- new experimental studies

- old experimental studies

- proposals for new experimental studies

- read-across

- (Quantitative) Structure-Activity Relationship [(Q)SAR]

- weight of evidence.

Data for the period up to March 2016 on the number of new and existing substances completing their data requirements via each of the above routes is described in the report entitled *The Use of Alternatives to Testing on Animals for the REACH Regulation* (ECHA, 2017).

Table B.1 provides a breakdown of the costs by endpoint. It also provides data on the average costs of new experimental studies drawn from the Risk & Policy Analysts Limited (RPA)'s in-house database of testing costs and the number of animals required to undertake tests.

Table B.1. **Endpoints, average costs of experimental studies and number of test animals required**

Endpoint	Number of animals required*	Average cost of experimental study (EUR)
Bioaccumulation	0	33 145
Short-term toxicity to fish	14	7 155
Long-term toxicity to fish	400	37 224
Long-term toxicity to birds	70	61 470
Toxicokinetics	60	1 300
Acute toxicity (all routes)	11	6 044
Skin irritation/corrosion	2	2 192
Eye irritation	2	1 647
Skin sensitisation	23	10 049
Repeated dose toxicity (all routes)	50	316 131
Genetic toxicity *in vitro*	0	11 402
Genetic toxicity *in vivo*	40	20 579
Carcinogenicity	400	1 210 128
Toxicity to reproduction	80	338 699
Developmental toxicity	100	112 191

* From Van der Jagt, K. et al. (2004).

These data have been used to derive estimates of the statistical average costs of new experimental studies and costs avoided owing to (Q)SARs via the OECD (Q)SAR Toolbox. These are provided in Table B.2.

For new industrial chemicals, costs are based on actual numbers of tests and (Q)SARs undertaken for new industrial chemicals registered in the EU and the average costs of experimental studies (as in Table B.1). In terms of costs avoided owing to (Q)SARs, it has been assumed that in the absence of a valid (Q)SAR or read-across, a new experimental study would be undertaken for all endpoints except the most expensive ones, namely repeated dose toxicity – all routes, carcinogenicity, toxicity to reproduction and developmental toxicity. For these endpoints it has been assumed that new experimental studies would only be carried out in 10% of cases where no (Q)SAR was available.

REACH requires different levels of information for substances manufactured or imported at different tonnages. As such, the level of information required for a given endpoint will differ from one tonnage to the next. Data from the European Chemical Agency's *Registration Database* (available at https://echa.europa.eu/information-on-chemicals/registered-substances) have been analysed to identify the number of substances requiring different levels (and costs) of individual tests (where they are required). These have been used to develop a statistical cost of new experimental studies and cost avoided by using (Q)SARs/read-across (employing the same assumptions above on the most expensive test endpoints in the absence of (Q)SARs/read-across).

Table B.2. **Average cost of testing for new and existing substances and savings owing to (Q)SARs**

	New substances	Existing substances
Average statistical cost of new experimental studies (EUR per substance)	169 531	80 740
Average statistical cost avoided via (Q)SARs/read-across (EUR per substance)[1]	20 545	30 162
Average cost per substance in the absence of (Q)SARs/read-across (EUR per substance)[2]	190 076	137 101
Average statistical test animals used (per substance)	76	46
Average statistical test animals avoided via (Q)SARs/read-across (per substance)	33	95

Notes:

1. These cost savings have been calculated on the assumption that in the absence of the OECD (Q)SAR Toolbox, experimental studies would otherwise need to be undertaken for all endpoints except the most expensive ones, namely repeated dose toxicity – all routes, carcinogenicity, toxicity to reproduction and developmental toxicity. For these endpoints it has been assumed that new experimental studies would only be carried out in 10% of cases where no (Q)SAR was available.

2. Costs for new substances are broadly comparable with the responses given on new substances in the 2018 EHS survey of industry (see Table A.2 in Annex A). The values in the table are used in the main analysis carried out by the RPA.

References

ECHA (2017), *The Use of Alternatives to Testing on Animals for the REACH Regulation*, Third report under Article 117(3) of the REACH Regulation, European Chemicals Agency, Helsinki, https://www.echa.europa.eu/documents/10162/13639/alternatives_test_animals_2017_en.pdf/075c690d-054c-693a-c921-f8cd8acbe9c3.

Van der Jagt, K. et al. (2004), "Alternative approaches can reduce the use of test animals under REACH", Addendum to the report "Assessment of additional testing needs under REACH: Effects of (Q)SARS, risk based testing and voluntary industry initiatives",

European Communities, Italy, http://publications.jrc.ec.europa.eu/repository/bitstream/JRC29111/EU
R%2021405%20EN.pdf.

Annex C. Countries and regions used in this report

One assumption used in the estimation of benefits from the Environment, Health and Safety (EHS) Programme in the 2010 *Cutting Costs in Chemicals Management* report (OECD, 2010) was that companies that conducted safety testing and registered a new chemical in one country also did so in other markets in the OECD. In response to a survey conducted in 2008, the industrial chemicals and pesticides industries responded that the average number of markets in which their products were marketed was three. (The number of regions was used in the calculation of the benefits of the Mutual Acceptance of Data [MAD] due to a reduction in duplicative testing to multiple regions.) These three regions correlated with the main OECD regions: Asia/Pacific, Europe and North America.

For the current volume, the industrial chemicals and pesticides industries, as well as the biocides industry, were asked the same question. As noted in Annex A, companies in each sector responded that the average number of markets in which their products were marketed were: industrial chemicals (3); pesticides (3.5) and biocides (3.5).

This range is in line with what would be expected given the increase in the number of countries that are members of the OECD and also non-member full adherents to the MAD system since the 2010 report was published. In particular, the number of OECD countries has grown from 30 to 37 (including Colombia[1]), and 6 non-members are now full adherents to MAD.

Table C.1 lists the number of countries in each region of the world – except from the three original OECD regions – that either became OECD member countries after 2010 (highlighted in bold) or that are non-member full adherents to MAD (marked with an asterix). Further, the table provides the percentage of gross domestic product (GDP) in a region accounted for by the new OECD countries and full adherents, so as to reflect their relative significance in the markets in which chemicals can be traded more easily thanks to MAD.

In summary, the table shows that the number of *new* OECD countries[2] or full adherents to MAD account for the following percentages of total GDP in their regions:

- Asia (17%)
- Latin America and the Carribean (79%)
- sub-Shaharan Africa (23%)
- Near East (16%).

Thus, it can reasonably be assumed that the number of regions in which industry benefits from MAD is between three and four.

Table C.1. **Countries and regions used in the report**

Region (member countries that joined the OECD post-2010 are highlighted in bold and non-member full adherents to MAD are marked with an asterix; member countries that joined before 2010 are not included)[1]	GDP in USD (World Bank, 2017)	Number of countries in the region	Percentage in the region of member countries that joined the OECD post-2010 and non-member full adherents to MAD	Percentage of regional GDP due to member countries that joined the OECD post 2010 and non-member full adherents to MAD
Asia (excluding Near East)	19 125 440 079 395	26	11.54%	16.92%
Afghanistan	20 815 300 220			
Bangladesh	249 723 887 765			
Bhutan	2 511 852 941			
Brunei Darussalam	12 128 089 002			
Cambodia	22 158 209 503			
China, People's Republic of	12 237 700 479375			
Hong Kong, China	341 449 340 451			
India*	2 597 491 162 898			
Indonesia	1 015 539 017 537			
Islamic Republic of Iran	439 513 511 621			
Democratic People's Republic of Korea	...			
Lao People's Democratic Republic	...			
Macau, China	50 361 201 096			
Malaysia*	314 500 279 044			
Maldives	4 597 083 304			
Mongolia	11 488 046 881			
Myanmar	69 322 122 756			
Nepal	24 472 013 234			
Pakistan	304 951 818 494			
Philippines	313 595 208 737			
Singapore*	323 907 234 412			
Sri Lanka	87 174 682 200			
Chinese Taipei	...			
Thailand	455 220 920 571			
Timor-Leste	2 954 621 000			
Viet Nam	223 863 996 355			
Latin America and Caribbean	3 821 042 135 166	44	9.09%	79%
Anguilla	...			
Antigua and Barbuda	1 532 397 556			
Argentina*	637 590 419 269			
Aruba	...			
Bahamas	12 162 100 000			
Barbados	4 796 845 981			
Belize	1 838 000 000			
Plurinational State of Bolivia	37 508 642 113			
Brazil*	2 055 505 502 225			
British Virgin Islands	...			
Cayman Islands	...			
Chile	277 076			
Colombia[1]	309 191 382 833			
Costa Rica	57 057 372 468			
Cuba	...			

Table C.1. **Countries and regions used in the report** (*continued*)

Region (member countries that joined the OECD post-2010 are highlighted in bold and non-member full adherents to MAD are marked with an asterix; member countries that joined before 2010 are not included)	GDP in USD (World Bank, 2017)	Number of countries in the region	Percentage in the region of member countries that joined the OECD post-2010 and non-member full adherents to MAD	Percentage of regional GDP due to member countries that joined the OECD post-2010 and non-member full adherents to MAD
Dominica	562 540 741			
Dominican Republic	75 931 656 815			
Ecuador	103 056 619 000			
El Salvador	24 805 439 600			
French Guiana	n.a.			
Grenada	1 118 816 679			
Guadeloupe	n.a.			
Guatemala	75 620 095 538			
Guyana	3 675 631 961			
Haiti	8 408 150 518			
Honduras	22 978 532 897			
Jamaica	14 768 134 912			
Martinique	n.a.			
Montserrat	n.a.			
Nicaragua	13 814 261 536			
Panama	61 838 175 800			
Paraguay	29 734 895 249			
Peru	211 389 272 242			
Puerto Rico	n.a.			
Saint Kitts and Nevis	n.a.			
Saint Lucia	n.a.			
Saint Vincent and the Grenadines	n.a.			
Suriname	n.a.			
Trinidad and Tobago	n.a.			
Turks and Caicos Islands	n.a.			
Uruguay	56 156 972 158			
Bolivarian Republic of Venezuela	n.a.			
British Virgin Islands	n.a.			
Sub-Saharan Africa	1 522 676	46	2%	23%
Angola	124 209			
Benin	9 274			
Botswana	17 407			
Burkina Faso	12 873			
Burundi	3 478			
Cabo Verde	1 754			
Cameroon	34 799			
Central African Republic	1 949			
Chad	9 981			
Comoros	649			
Democratic Republic of Congo	37 241			
Republic of the Congo	8 723			
Côte d'Ivoire	40 389			

Table C.1. **Countries and regions used in the report** (*continued*)

Region (member countries that joined the OECD post-2010 are highlighted in bold and non-member full adherents to MAD are marked with an asterix; member countries that joined before 2010 are not included)	GDP in USD (World Bank, 2017)	Number of countries in the region	Percentage in the region of member countries that joined the OECD post-2010 and non-member full adherents to MAD	Percentage of regional GDP due to member countries that joined the OECD post-2010 and non-member full adherents to MAD
Equatorial Guinea	12 487			
Eritrea	n.a.			
Ethiopia	80 562			
Gabon	14 623			
Gambia	1 015			
Ghana	47 330			
Guinea	10 491			
Guinea-Bissau	1 347			
Kenya	74 938			
Lesotho	2 639			
Liberia	2 158			
Madagascar	11 500			
Malawi	6 303			
Mali	15 288			
Mauritania	5 025			
Mauritius	13 338			
Mozambique	12 334			
Namibia	13 245			
Niger	8 120			
Nigeria	375 771			
Rwanda	9 137			
Sao Tome & Principe	391			
Senegal	16 375			
Seychelles	1 486			
Sierra Leone	3 774			
South Africa*	349 419			
South Sudan	n.a.			
Swaziland	4 409			
United Republic of Tanzania	52 090			
Togo	4 813			
Uganda	25 891			
Zambia	25 809			
Zimbabwe	17 846			
Near East	2 138 712	14	7%	16%
Bahrain	35 307			
Cyprus[3,4]	21 652			
Iraq	197 716			
Israel	350 851			
Jordan	40 068			
Kuwait	120 126			
Lebanon	51 844			
Oman	72 643			
Qatar	167 605			
Saudi Arabia	683 827			
Syrian Arab Republic	n.a.			

Table C.1. **Countries and regions used in the report** (*continued*)

Region (member countries that joined the OECD post-2010 are highlighted in bold and non-member full adherents to MAD are marked with an asterix; member countries that joined before 2010 are not included)	GDP in USD (World Bank, 2017)	Number of countries in the region	Percentage in the region of member countries that joined the OECD post-2010 and non-member full adherents to MAD	Percentage of regional GDP due to member countries that joined the OECD post-2010 and non-member full adherents to MAD
United Arab Emirates	382 575			
West Bank and Gaza Strip	14 498			
Yemen	n.a.			

Notes

1. OECD countries agreed to invite Colombia to become a member of the Organisation and Colombia's membership will take effect after it has taken the appropriate steps at the national level to accede to the OECD Convention and deposited its instrument of accession with the French government, the depository of the Convention.

2. The table does not include the new members Estonia, Latvia, Lithuania and Slovenia, which joined the OECD from 2010 onwards, as they are part of the region "Europe" which was already accounted for in the 2010 *Cutting Costs in Chemicals Management* report (OECD, 2010).

3. Note by Turkey: The information in this document with reference to "Cyprus" relates to the southern part of the Island. There is no single authority representing both Turkish and Greek Cypriot people on the Island. Turkey recognises the Turkish Republic of Northern Cyprus (TRNC). Until a lasting and equitable solution is found within the context of the United Nations, Turkey shall preserve its position concerning the "Cyprus issue".

4. Note by all the European Union Member States of the OECD and the European Union: The Republic of Cyprus is recognised by all members of the United Nations with the exception of Turkey. The information in this document relates to the area under the effective control of the Government of the Republic of Cyprus.

References

OECD (2010), *Cutting Costs in Chemicals Management: How OECD Helps Governments and Industry*, OECD, Paris, https://doi.org/10.1787/9789264085930-en.

World Bank (2017), "GDP (current US$), https://data.worldbank.org/indicator/NY.GDP.MKTP.CD?view=map (accessed 1 July 2018).

ORGANISATION FOR ECONOMIC CO-OPERATION AND DEVELOPMENT

The OECD is a unique forum where governments work together to address the economic, social and environmental challenges of globalisation. The OECD is also at the forefront of efforts to understand and to help governments respond to new developments and concerns, such as corporate governance, the information economy and the challenges of an ageing population. The Organisation provides a setting where governments can compare policy experiences, seek answers to common problems, identify good practice and work to co-ordinate domestic and international policies.

The OECD member countries are: Australia, Austria, Belgium, Canada, Chile, the Czech Republic, Denmark, Estonia, Finland, France, Germany, Greece, Hungary, Iceland, Ireland, Israel, Italy, Japan, Korea, Latvia, Lithuania, Luxembourg, Mexico, the Netherlands, New Zealand, Norway, Poland, Portugal, the Slovak Republic, Slovenia, Spain, Sweden, Switzerland, Turkey, the United Kingdom and the United States. The European Union takes part in the work of the OECD.

OECD Publishing disseminates widely the results of the Organisation's statistics gathering and research on economic, social and environmental issues, as well as the conventions, guidelines and standards agreed by its members.

OECD PUBLISHING, 2, rue André-Pascal, 75775 PARIS CEDEX 16
(97 2019 04 1 P) ISBN 978-92-64-31170-1 – 2019

Printed by Libri Plureos GmbH in Hamburg,
Germany